SONSHIP

SONSHIP

ESSENTIAL WRITINGS FROM ERIC GILMOUR

TALL PINE

Sonship: Essential Writings from Eric Gilmour

Copyright © 2019 by Eric Gilmour

All rights reserved solely by the author. The author guarantees all contents are original and do not infringe upon the legal rights of any other person or work. No part of this book may be reproduced in any form without the permission of the author. The views expressed in this book are not necessarily those of the publisher.

Unless otherwise indicated, Bible quotations are taken from the New King James Version®. Copyright © 1982 by Thomas Nelson. Used by permission. All rights reserved. Scripture quotations designated NIV are from The Holy Bible, New International Version ® Copyright © 1973. 1978, 1984, 2011 by Biblica, Inc.; Scripture taken from The Message. Copyright © 1993, 1994, 1995, 1996, 2000, 2001, 2002. Used by permission of NavPress Publishing Group; Scripture designated CJB is taken from the Complete Jewish Bible by David H. Stern. Copyright © 1998. All rights reserved. Used by permission of Messianic Jewish Publishers, 6120 Day Long Lane, Clarksville, MD 21029. www. messianicjewish.net. Scripture quotations marked MSG are taken from THE MESSAGE, copyright © 1993, 1994, 1995, 1996, 2000, 2001, 2002 by Eugene H. Peterson. Used by permission of NavPress. All rights reserved. Represented by Tyndale House Publishers, Inc.

ISBN-13: 9781082221774 *(paperback)*

ISBN: 978-0-578-56660-3 *(hard cover)*

Tall Pine Books: An Imprint of Pulpit to Page
|| tallpinebooks.com
|| pulpittopage.com

CONTENTS

Foreword   xi

PART I
MARY OF BETHANY

1. If You Don't Let Me Kiss You...   3
2. She Loved Me.   7
3. You, Lord.   11

PART II
HOW TO BE HAPPY

4. The Infusion of Joy   15
5. God Wants You to Be Happy   17
6. Happily Enjoy All the Details of Your Life.   21
7. God Does Not Heal the Heart by Theology   25

PART III
NOSTALGIA

8. The Vision of Hosea   31
9. Prophets are Conduits   33
10. The Vision of the Locked Door   35
11. Withdrawing with God   39
12. Christ Teaches What He Is   41

PART IV
HOW TO PROSPER IN EVERYTHING

13. Maturity is Enjoying God   45
14. The Vision of the Light Being   47
15. Feeling God   49

PART V
UNION

16. Becoming True   57
17. Let Him Hold You   59

18. If you seek Me for power...   63
19. Chief Luminary   65

PART VI
INTO THE CLOUD

20. One thing is Necessary   71
21. Separation   75
22. Direct Contact   79
23. Abraham: Friendship with God   83
24. Moses, Aaron, and Samuel   87
25. The Key to Unlocking America   93
26. Am I Not Worth More to You than 10 sons?   95
27. A Caution on Identity   103

PART VII
ENJOYING THE GOSPEL

28. The Vision of the Trenching Shovel   109
29. The Offering of God's Presence to Men   111
30. Experience   115
31. Life   119
32. Presence   121
33. Communion   123

PART VIII
CONVERSATIONS ON DIVINE LIFE

34. The Presence of God is in the Present   127
35. Anointed One   129
36. Delight will Swallow Discipline   131
37. Our Father   133

PART IX
NAKED TRUST

38. Presenting the Lord   137
39. Am I Enough for You?   139
40. When God is Silent   141
41. Holy Complacency   143
42. Better than Saul   147
43. Simeon: A Listening Life   149

PART X
LOVESICK

44. Open to Me	153
45. He Waits for Us	157
46. Yielding to His Invitation	159
47. My First Vision of the Lord	163
48. God Grabbed my Chin	167
49. Marry Me	169
50. An Infection of Affection	171

PART XI
BURN

51. Will You Be Dominated?	177
52. Sonship	179
53. Intimacy	183
54. Only Jesus	185
55. Presenting the Fullness of Christ	189
56. The Church	193
57. The Problem in Coming Together	197
58. Take Up Your Cross	201
59. Repentance	205
60. A Manifestation of Oil	209
About the Author	211
Also By	213

Here lies my heart
Wicked
Wounded
Weary
Deeply sank, ruined and blank
Redeem me again
Esteem me Your friend
Lean in and mend
My broken love
Cover me
Take me up with Thee
Smother me
To recovery
Like there's no other but me
Let our eyes meet
As I lay on Your feet
Keep me
Completely
To finish from start
Heart upon heart
Help me cling to You
Sing to You
Linger in You
And bring to You
Everything I do.

—*Eric Gilmour*
Ontario, Canada
Summer 2019

FOREWORD

A few years ago, I found myself facedown on the hardwood floor of my living room. I was laying there in a puddle of tears as relief washed over me. I could not recall when this presence of peace had begun slipping away from me; but I was so overwhelmed with gratitude to feel rest returning to my heart again. How many months had it been since I was surrounded with God's embrace in this way? I remembered that this feeling was identical to how it had felt when I first met Jesus. I told myself I never wanted to lose this "place" again. I asked God to help me "live here", and to never let me move from it.

My laptop was open on the couch nearby. A man on the other side of the screen was preaching a message on Jesus as our Husband: looking at us and asking us if He was truly enough for us [*"Am I not worth more to you than 10 sons?"*]. I had never heard this preacher speak before, but his words were dripping with God, and it was as if they were reaching through the screen to grab ahold of me. I just kept playing the Youtube video over and over, and putting myself back on the ground to lay in God's kindness and nearness.

Only a few hours before this took place, I had been

standing in a public high school gymnasium preaching the Gospel to bleachers full of students. Many of the kids gave their lives to Jesus that day too. I had even had a dream of something to incorporate into my message the night before. By ministry standards, this had felt like a really successful day. I will never forget walking out to my car and driving home though. The drive felt horrible. My ministry high dissipated so quickly. I sat in my driveway for a while with my mind going in circles. I had just "heard God", and been "used by God", and saw Him "move through me"; "people were saved". And yet, here I was feeling so empty and sad. Where was joy? What was I doing wrong? I felt like I had been obedient to what God invited me to do. So how could I feel so "off" right now?

When I went inside, I started scrolling through Youtube videos of my favorite preachers looking for help. I wanted encouragement. I wanted wisdom beyond myself. Eventually, I ended up clicking on a video that popped up on the side of my screen. I decided to let it play through....and wow, I am so glad it happened to be Christ speaking to me through Eric Gilmour. As you read above, it ushered me into the moment where Jesus the Bridegrooom stepped into my life and introduced His loving jealousy to me upon Eric's voice. I have never been the same.

Soon after, I bought all of Eric's books and read them nonstop. Through Eric's pen, the Lord began teaching me the beauty of Union, stillness before Him in the prayer closet, and the delight of continually beholding Jesus. I found a depth of intimacy I didn't know I could have. I slipped my iPad between the pages of my college textbooks and read Eric's ebooks through all my university classes. I also awkwardly began crying in public places at inopportune times when God's voice would suddenly fall on me or I would sense His touch. I found myself hiding in my car throughout the day, just to be alone with Jesus for a few moments. The testimonies and experiences Eric includes in his writings unveiled God's nature and character to me in ways I had never heard of. Some of the wonders he shares even began multiplying into my own life.

As you encounter the same loving Christ in these writings, I believe an inevitable lovesickness will begin to pour into you too. This is what the kiss of God's presence and voice does to people. So many of Jesus' present-speaking words to His Church are laced within these very pages. Therefore, the messages you will find compiled in this book carry Christ's own presence and power to touch and remold the human heart. I know they continue to soften and reshape mine. I am honored to lay before you the portions that have impacted me most.

—Bre Buxton
Orlando, FL
July 2019

I

MARY OF BETHANY

1

IF YOU DON'T LET ME KISS YOU...

HAVE YOU EVER SAID SOMETHING TO SOMEONE IN conversation, and suddenly God takes your exact words and throws them back at you? I remember a time when God grabbed words I spoke and spoke them right back to me. I was playing around with my daughter and trying to tackle her before bed. I said playfully, "If you don't let me kiss you, there is no way for you to love me!" I tried again, "Baby, if you don't let me kiss you, there's no way for you to love me!"

God took my words, redirected them, and spoke to me by them: "Eric, if you don't let me kiss you, there's no way for you to love me." What does that mean? You *have* to be touched! You *have* to be kissed! You have to be held! You must know the sweet, intimate touch that takes place behind closed doors! All of the public things are wonderful, but the reason for them is for us to fall in love with Him! Oh, that we would know what it is to go into the King's chamber and be thrilled beyond imagination! There is no higher delight! I'm so thrilled to share with you this key to *happiness*, the root of peace, and the bliss of life. Bliss, peace, and joy...such things are *yours* because they *are* Him—and He has given Himself to you!

I want to share some truths with you that might seem contrary to many things which you've heard; however, they aren't contrary at all. In fact, these truths *lie beneath* much of what you've heard.

My heart is this: that our greatest take-away from our time in ministry meetings and church settings would be that when we go home and go back to normal life, we would experience the reality of His person in our daily lives. That's the main concern. It's my focal point and life mission. Some people fall into traps because they attend powerful, Holy Ghost- filled meetings, but then they go back to work on Monday. They change diapers on Tuesday. They are shuffling papers on Wednesday. They're working with a difficult boss or perhaps they're being tried by a tough marriage. In all these things, what we find *in Him* must stay relevant and active. We often observe the lives of great men of God and great people of stature and measure ourselves by them.

It's tempting to think that what *we* have is not relevant compared to others' giftings. We think, "Well, there is no way I can pack out a stadium like so-and-so. There is no way I can minister like this person or that person. There's no way I can be as successful as them." This is perverse thinking. We must change the definition of *success* in our hearts.

Success is not miracles. Success is not preaching. Success is not people falling out in the Spirit. It's not riches and it's not fame. Do you want to know what success is? Success is a heart that is captivated by the love of Jesus.

There's a scary area of scripture where the Bible mentions how many will come to Jesus in the end saying, "Lord, Lord, did we not...?" And in essence, Jesus responds with, "You didn't have a kiss with me. You may have had public encounters, but you had no private kiss."

Oh, if you don't let Him kiss you, there's no way for you to love Him! If you've ever touched Him, you know that He has one thing on His mind in that moment: *holding you*. When you allow Him to hold you, He somehow *drains out* all of your inward poisons: bitterness, selfish ambition, anger, lusts...He drains them out when you simply let Him hold you. This, to me, is the secret of *everything*.

2

SHE LOVED ME.

"T̲ʀᴜʟʏ I ᴛᴇʟʟ ʏᴏᴜ, ᴡʜᴇʀᴇᴠᴇʀ ᴛʜɪs ɢᴏsᴘᴇʟ ɪs ᴘʀᴇᴀᴄʜᴇᴅ throughout the world, what she has done will also be told, in memory of her." Matthew 26:13 (NIV)

This means that Jesus wanted Mary of Bethany to be *remembered*. If that's true, then she must be significant! Not only that, He tied the memory of her to the global spread of the gospel! At first, this bothered me, because I thought to myself, she never preached a message. She never taught a class. She never wrote a book. She never performed any miracles.

She is only mentioned three times in scripture. I said, "Lord, what could it be in this woman that would cause her to be tied to the testimony of Your name for all time? What is it that's so special to You?"

As I waited, I heard His voice. He said, "She *loved* me." It doesn't sound significant, does it? I thought, "Lord, so many people have loved You! What makes *her* different?" I realized that God took me to this passage to show me the *kind* of love that she had, which separated her from so many others. The *kind* of love that she had was intrinsic to the spread of the gospel!

Luke 10:38, the first mention of this woman, describes her like this: "She sat at His feet, listening to His words." Isn't that beautiful? Think of this picture: a crowded house full of commotion...and then there is this woman. She is on her knees and, with fixed eyes, she is steadily staring at Him. It's the first mention of this precious woman. If I had been there, I would have been struck by her magnificent obsession. It would have hit me hard. Why? Because she didn't care what anyone thought of her. She was looking at Him. This is the life I want! To gaze upon the Lamb who was slain.

She teaches us something so significant. She teaches us that He Himself is too beautiful to look away from. She teaches us that there is actually honey dripping forth from His lips. *That* honey which drips from His lips is sweet to our taste!

"Gracious words are a honeycomb, sweet to the soul and healing to the bones." Proverbs 16:24 (NIV)

"Know also that wisdom is like honey for you..." Proverbs 24:14 (NIV)

I see that the story of Mary of Bethany is a call to be captivated by Him! She is a demonstration of His worth. She is a proclamation of the preeminence of His person.

Her love cries out that He is greater than His gifts! He is more wonderful than His wonders! Stare at Him for He is greater than the anointing. He is lovely. She wasn't standing in awe of His powers. She had found something so much more valuable. She found that He Himself was the fulfillment of her soul, the satisfaction and joy of her life.

She was struck breathless by the overwhelming conviction that He is more lovely than anything she had seen. She realized that being with Him was to have everything she had ever wanted, it was to be everything she ever wanted to be, and it was to arrive everywhere she had ever dreamed of going. She found that His presence freed her from the need to have anything else. Most of all, she found that her prayers had vanished simply by His presence. How? Because she found that He was and is everything she needed and everything she ever wanted.

His presence transformed the mundane and common house that she lived in into a garden of spices with her beloved. She drew near. Near enough to hear, if nothing else, His breathing.

"When the eyes of the soul looking out meet the eyes of God looking in, heaven has begun right here on earth." —AW Tozer

Many of you might think, "I don't know this life." Let me tell you, Jesus described this life as "the good part." He went on to describe it as untouchable and eternal! Following that, He said it is "the *one thing* that is needed." In other words, "the *only* necessity in life is right here, looking at Me."

Mary shows us that the essential Christian message is not to behave, but to behold. You can tell who doesn't *really* want God to rule their lives by who doesn't take time to simply sit and listen to Him.

3

YOU, LORD.

I was at an event in which prayers and outcries were being offered profusely to the Lord. In the midst of the meeting, I was taken up in a vision, and as I overlooked the room, I saw that all of the prayers going up were all one specific color. However, there was one person who had prayers going up that were a different color than all of the rest.

In the vision, I was able to hone in on the one person's prayer, and as I leaned in, I heard the person saying, "You, You, You! I want You, oh Lord!" The Lord wants us to sanctify His name. He desires that His name be lifted up and picked up higher and higher than the rest—because He is more lovely and beautiful. He will literally blind us to everything else. Our simple adoration and desire for Him and Him alone sets our prayers apart from mere petition.

So here in the story, Mary comes to Jesus. Her brother has died. Her heart is hurting and she doesn't understand. What does she do? She throws herself at His feet. Can you see why she was so special to Him? Everyone else is standing up and talking. They have opinions about this and that and plenty of unanswered questions. Yet what does Mary do? She throws everything and herself at His feet. An act that professes, "You, Lord, are more lovely and worthy to me than all the answers and facts that I could find!"

Here is the problem: men would rather explain than adore. They would rather inquire than simply adore. Mary shows us that she is willing to worship Him despite not understanding. Certainly she had feelings and thoughts and questions about the situation— yet she was willing to throw them down, along with her own life, at the feet of Jesus. She is literally saying that Christ's presence is more important than answers.

I don't know what you're going through or what you've been through, but I know that He Himself is better than any answer He could give you. Too often we get distracted by what He gives and we begin to come to Him for something other than Him...and we wonder why we keep missing the sweet, blissful enjoyment of His person!

Even though Mary and Martha had similar discussions with Jesus, He responded with resurrection power to Mary only. Do you see this? Mary shows us that she would rather move Him than understand Him. She was more interested in touching Him than defining Him. She shows us that something takes place in adoration that makes understanding not that important anymore. The memory of her, which is intrinsic to the gospel, is God's invitation for all to love Him as she loved Him. She is the embodiment of the first commandment.

II

HOW TO BE HAPPY

4

THE INFUSION OF JOY

GOD WANTS TO GIVE YOU A *GIFT*. OF COURSE, HE WANTS TO give many...but allow me to dial in this teaching on a specific gift. As I do, remember something about a gift: it has nothing to do with you. In other words, all you must do is receive. Your merit doesn't release it; His goodness does. There are no hoops to jump through or special requirements. Red tape isn't the language of the Kingdom.

To be specific, I feel that the Lord is releasing the gift of *joy* on the body of Christ, because it's so desperately needed. We have a serious joy famine on our hands...may this work remedy that. Many people deal with a *real* sense of heaviness. They become scattered in their minds. Excess *thinking* becomes normal. These things ought not be.

When we wait on the Lord, it pulls the Word to us. David said, "I wait for your word..." (Psalm 119:74). In other words, the *Word* comes through *waiting*. If we would take time to simply wait on Him, we would receive His Word. Why do people have no clue what God is saying? They simply won't *wait*. If the Word travels to me on the path of my own waiting...then I'll surely experience a famine of Word in my life if I allow busyness to eliminate the simple art of *waiting*.

Waiting is taking the time to give God all of your attention. It's a *turning* of your attention, if you will. Impatience is often the very thing that steals our attention and doesn't allow us to wait on the Lord. *Impatience is an idol factory*. If you don't want to wait on God and you decide to go do *something else,* you will absolutely fashion something else in His place. Remember when Moses went to the mountain and Israel became restless? They fashioned an idol in His place and they even named the idol "Yahweh."

You can name your idol whatever you'd like. You could name it something spiritual or positive sounding. At the end of the day, it's still an object that is wrongfully taking the place of God. It's simple: if the origin is off, the whole thing is off. If our hearts are producing a dark thing, we can't give it a pretty enough label to redeem it. If it counters the will of God for our attention to be fixed on Him, it isn't worthy of our focus.

Impatience is disinterest in the Dove. Let me explain. Remember, Noah let the first bird out and then the second and he waited for the return of the *dove*. If we won't wait for the Dove (the Spirit), we become disinterested. We are more into our own plans. If our hearts aren't laid at His feet, they always try to take His seat. It's the human disposition to try to take His place.

However, when we wait upon Him, we give Him His proper throne in our hearts. If we choose not to wait and be still, we are actually saying, "I've got this. I don't need You to rule me. I'll go forward saying all the right things and sounding the part, but I don't need Your actual reign in my life." The interesting thing is, if we lay at His feet, He actually calls us to sit with Him (see Ephesians 2:6). Yet, if we try to be seated on the throne apart from Him, our attempt is futile.

5

GOD WANTS YOU TO BE HAPPY

I got away by myself and entered a small prayer chapel to give my attention to Him. I became quiet and still before the Lord. Notice both the quietness and the stillness. *Quietness is the absence of external noise. Stillness is the absence of internal noise.* So many people become quiet in their surroundings but are filled with noise internally, thus they have no stillness. This is key, because our instruction is not to merely be quiet, but to be still. What we really need in order to hear the Lord is to remove ourselves from the hurricane outside and to remove the hurricane on the inside!

As I sat in quietness and stillness in the chapel, I felt the Lord speak something to me. I actually saw in a flash the R&B group called 112 out of the blue. I remembered them and thought, "Whoa, the Lord must be saying something to me." I instantly remembered Joel 1:12 which says, "The people's joy is withered away" (NIV). I've found that the majority of Christians whom my wife and I know have no joy whatsoever. They may have lots of "revelation," but no joy. They might have a big ministry and they might have it together on the outside, but totally lack genuine joy on the inside.

Andrew Murray said, "If the hands on the clock are not ticking, you know there is an internal problem." Likewise, if joy is not present in the life of a believer, you know there is an internal problem. Obviously, there is an attack in this area in the body of Christ. The attack isn't necessarily on joy itself, but it's an attack on our connection to the vine! The evidence of your connection being attacked is a lack of joy. Your joy levels can be used as a measuring stick for your connection with Jesus!

Let me just clear the air...God wants you to be happy! All my life, I've heard different things than that. I've heard that God is not interested in my happiness. I've now learned that He wants me to be so happy, not in stuff and things, but in Him.

He wants me to be happy in my reality! So often, people are caught placing their happiness in un-reality.

"But when He, the Spirit of truth, comes..." (John 16:13). The translation for the word truth in this passage is actually the word reality in the original text. "When He, the Spirit of reality, comes..."

He shows us what is real and what is not real. So many can't decide what's real and what's fake. The Holy Spirit enables us to decipher the difference. What is real to God? It's the thing that lasts forever! What's real to Him is that which comes from Him, lasts forever, and never began! That is reality to God. The Spirit of reality has come to show you what is real...what came from God, what lasts forever, and what has no beginning! He came to show us the eternality of God, if you will.

It doesn't get anymore real than the fact that a connection to the joyful vine cannot produce anything but a joyful branch. Our beings haven't come into distance contact with a joyful King but have literally been infused with His joyful

Spirit. This isn't just demeanor-altering truth but nature altering reality.

6

HAPPILY ENJOY ALL THE DETAILS OF YOUR LIFE.

OFTEN WHAT STOPS US FROM DRINKING DEEP IS THINKING DEEP. We focus so much on what this person says or what that person thinks and it hinders us from simply drinking of the Lord fully. It's time to not give a rip about the opinions of those around us, but simply place the chalice of God to our lips and allow Him in.

I was once in the closet drinking of Him, and as I did, I slipped into a vision. In the vision, Jesus had a *massive* paintbrush dripping with red paint. He was dragging it behind Him and walking toward me. I am looking at Him, unsure of what He is about to do to me. Suddenly, He took this massive paintbrush and smeared it across my face and painted a big smile on my face. He then grabbed me and brought me face-to-face with Him and said, "Happily enjoy all the details of your life!" This changed me forever! He wants to anoint you with the oil of gladness!

He wants to put upon you the oil of joy so that through face-to-face contact with Him, you can enjoy every aspect of your life! You might think, "Well, Eric, there are a lot of aspects of my life that are not enjoyable!"

That might be true; however, He is with you in them all and thereby provides joy *through* it all! The scriptures say, "Therefore God, your God, has anointed you. With the oil of gladness above your companions" (Hebrews 1:9). In other words, there wasn't another man as joyful as Jesus.

Some might say, "Well, sure, but that was for Jesus... not us." Then we must look at another scripture in which Jesus said, "These things I have spoken to you so that my joy may be in you, and *that* your joy may be made full" (John 15:11, emphasis added). The joy of Jesus is sharable.

"You have put gladness in my heart" (Psalm 4:7). See, God places joy within us. It's His heart in us. Martin Luther once wrote, "I know how easily one can forfeit the joy of the gospel." It's quite easy to forget how joyful this life really is! We've failed to remember that in the midst of everything, we can experience joy unspeakable by drinking of Him. I don't share these things to tickle ears or to give a shallow encouragement.

I share the message of joy with a deep-rooted conviction that God is going to break joy open over us in a much needed way. It will change everything about our lives! Joy isn't just an idea, but an actual, tangible fruit of God's Spirit!

"In your presence is fullness of joy..." (Psalm 16:11). What does fullness of joy mean? It means there is no area that isn't touched with joy. Mother Teresa once said, "A joyful face preaches without preaching."

I think often we disqualify ourselves when we try to preach the joyful good news of glad tidings without being touched by joy!

How can we preach glad tidings when we ourselves are not glad? When you as a person are dipped into the fullness of God's joy, you will attract people. Folks will want to listen to what you have to say simply because you're smiling so much. If Jesus *really* did die for us and if He *really* did set us free, then an eruption of internal joy can only be the byproduct.

"Restore to me the joy of your salvation" (Psalm 51:12). In other words, the salvation that you have has got joy *sewn* into it. You separate yourselves from the wonderful victories of salvation when you cease drinking of the joy which is Himself. Are you being convinced yet of the happy intention of God?

In the scriptures, *wine* and *joy* are mixed together. "And wine which makes man's heart glad, So that he may make his face glisten with oil" (Psalm 104:15). God literally gifts wine as a gift which is representative of His Spirit. What is the result of drinking of His spirit? Gladness of heart!

Yet it doesn't stop there... He gives reason for this gift: "So that he may make his face glisten with oil." What does it mean to glisten with oil? It's the Spirit of God coming out of your countenance! It's displaying the Person of the Lord. It's bearing His image!

As these things happen and take shape in our lives, we are able to preach without preaching. Of course, we should continue to preach the gospel verbally, without question.However, with joy on our countenance, there is a preaching that happens in passing someone on the street. Your spouse needs to see a face that's glistening with oil in their lives. Your children need to look up to mom and dad and see a face glistening with oil! Your friends need a friend to look to with a face glistening with oil! This glistening will only happen through joy in the heart which comes from drinking of the Lord.

7

GOD DOES NOT HEAL THE HEART BY THEOLOGY

...BUT BY WINE.

The intoxication of God causes such joy! It's for you today, it's for you later, it's for you always! I'm simply reminding you of things that you already know! It's not just a holly jolly Christmas, but a holly jolly life!

In Isaiah 9:3 we see that Jesus increases joy, "You have increased their joy." Oh how the church needs an increase of joy. I need it. You need it. Jesus alone can give it. The Psalms give us quite an education in this joy that God gives to men. David writes, "You have put joy in my heart." Psalm 4:7 He goes on to say where His joy comes from and how we can receive.

Joy is in taking refuge in God. Psalm 5:1
Joy is in His presence. Psalm 16:11
Joy is resting in His victory. Psalm 20:5
Joy is connected to righteous living. Psalm 30:11
God is Joy. Psalm 33:1
Joy is in His rule. Psalm 43:14
Joy is in hearing Him. Psalm 48:2
Joy is in repentance. Psalm 51:8,12

Joy is in His shadow. Psalm 63:7
Joy is in His presence. Psalm 84:2
Joy is the Springs of God. Psalm 87:7
Joy is our satisfaction. Psalm 90:14
Joy is in the presence of God, Psalm 95:2

Paul shows us that joy is shed abroad in our hearts, by the Holy Spirit. In Romans 15:30 he is telling the Romans that the Holy Spirit burst your heart open with joy. Richard Rolle wrote about this joy in no uncertain terms, "I feel I will die in the face of your joy." Have you ever seen anyone write this way before? He is saying, "I am so joyful that I feel I am going to die." Catherine of Sienna wrote, "I am so filled with joy I am surprised that my soul stays in my body." I am writing this book to tell you that it is for you. It is God's will that you be animated with joy in His presence. It is going to come through drinking. I can hear people saying, "Eric, you don't understand, such and such just happened." I say to you, use that situation as another window to pass into God and enjoy Him.

Paul was so convinced of this evidence of the Spirit that he told the Thessalonians that joy is our way of life. (see 1 Thessalonians 5:16) Not some of the time, but "rejoice always." Not just sometimes. All the time. You may say, "Eric, you don't know all the trials going on in my life. James has a good answer for that, "Consider it all joy, my brethren when you encounter various trials" (James 1:2). It is as if he is saying, "In all your trials be joy-filled. See all your trials as an avenue to share in the joy of His presence." In fact, the strength in your trial is tied to the joy you have in it. Nehemiah 8 shows us that joy is our strength. It is the result of the Spirit in Galatians 5:22. The work of the Spirit and the gospel in the world is inseparable from "The Spirit of the Lord is upon me, because the Lord has anointed me...to grant those who mourn in

Zion, giving them a garland instead of ashes, the old of joy instead of mourning" (Isaiah 61:1-3).

The presence of God in the person of the Holy Spirit will banish mourning and depression. He will lift the oppression and break the heaviness off of your life and replace it with a lifted heart of joy. Oh many of your hearts are hurting. You feel damaged on the inside because of something you have done, or something someone has done to you. You feel pain inside from weariness and dryness. God does not heal the heart by theology. He heals it by wine. When the New Wine of heaven enters, the old religious wineskins burst! May all the weights fall off of your life as you enter the joy of His presence. May your home be filled with joy. May your marriage be filled with joy. May your relationships be filled with joy... joy of such a kind that even on your way to be martyred, your heart will sing of His unfailing love and beauty.

III
NOSTALGIA

8

THE VISION OF HOSEA

HIS FACE WAS MADE OF STONE AND THE EXPRESSION ON HIS FACE was deep brokenness. I knew in my spirit that his brokenhearted anguish was a fracture of the kind that only betrayed lovers know. He wasn't God; he was a human possessed with God's feelings. He, himself, in his own body bore God's emotions. By grace the Lord brought the personification of His current feelings to me through this vision and image of this prophet. In the vision I knew by intuition that this prophet of stone in front of me was Hosea.

Why was he made of stone? I am not sure. Though in other instances the Lord gave messages to prophets and told them that He would make their faces like flint (stone) to break the hardness in His people. I can only speculate that this is what God was trying to communicate to me. Hosea's burden, heart, and message would be relayed and would require a face like flint to break the hardness of His people.

Prior to this experience, the Spirit had pulled me into a series of profound illuminations through Hosea's prophetic record. Though the Lord restricted me from speaking of the things that He showed me in those days, I knew that to communicate them would one day be required of me. For over three years I waited. Then, this vision of a stone Hosea, at the turn of this year (2016), marks what I believe is a distinct disclosing of God's heart toward His people in this time.

Father, let these feeble letters press into the souls of Your people an image of Your broken heart over a church whose hearts have fallen in love with other things. Those who have forgotten You. Those who have forsaken the love exchange they once shared with You.

Dear reader, many prophets have uttered God's words as divine mouthpieces but none have pictured for us God's broken heart like what we have seen in Hosea. For though others cry, "Injustice!" "Transgression!" or "Wickedness!"

Hosea's nostalgic cry is simply, "You don't love Me anymore."

9

PROPHETS ARE CONDUITS

IN ANY PEERING INTO PROPHETIC WRITINGS IT IS EASY TO NOTE that the lives and words of the prophets are connected to the days in which they are living. In this day, God breathes into the soul of Hosea His own anguish as Hosea's personal life is turmoiled by a like agony. As the prophet receives God's words into him, he inevitably becomes God's communication to men. It was God's speaking into Hosea coupled with Hosea's obedience that brought Hosea into union with what God was communicating of Himself to him.

It is important to understand that prophets are conduits. They are simply the means of God's message. Hosea embodies God's current heartbreak over a people who have covenanted with Him yet refuse to love Him. He has come into covenant with a woman who refuses loving-faithfulness. Though the prophets themselves personify their divine communication, Hosea's union with his holy relay is unique and arguably the clearest image of God's wounded heart, outside of Christ Himself.

Dear reader, take note. If you feel that such prophetic things are God's desire for your life, you will be united with

God's feelings in the same way that Hosea was...God speaking into your soul. If God's voice isn't penetrating your heart you will never be pierced with His feelings. If you wish for a prophetic life you must share both the ecstasy of God and the agony of God. It is in the enjoyment of His ecstasy that you are enabled to receive and properly steward God's agony. In the name "Hosea" ecstasy and agony had found a home. Are you willing to house the same? If God gives Himself to us He will unite our hearts with His agony through the beatific experience of Himself.

Notice the last four words of the text. These are the words used to describe the harlotry of God's people, "departing from the Lord." The things that they are doing outwardly are only a fruit of a distance inwardly. To depart from the person and presence of God is the root of harlotry. If a man departs from God he loses the source of everything divine in his life: the will to obey, the sense to obey, the love for God, and even the power that comes from God.

The actions of harlotry are inevitable in a person's life whose heart has left God's presence. God must be first priority. This means that His presence is paramount. If He remains first in the heart, then harlotry can never enter it. If He is eclipsed in any form or fashion, the seed of harlotry sneaks in. The moment that we erect an idol its lifelessness begins to pass into us. This is why harlotry breeds death; man has departed from Life Himself.

10

THE VISION OF THE LOCKED DOOR

"*I shall go after my lovers who give me bread...*" (Hosea 2:7)

THE SPIRITUAL DECEPTION BLINDING THE SPIRITUAL ADULTERER is that other things will satisfy. The adultery in the church is fueled by this tiny lie: that a man can be satisfied apart from God's presence and voice—that there is bread for the soul that did not come out of heaven; that there is drink outside of the River of Life the flows out from under the throne of God (rule of God). So because of this we have gone on and into things other than God Himself. We have exited His loving rule and sat ourselves upon the throne.

Many have survived by services, small groups, house meetings, or some other thing, but growth in the knowing of God has hardly been realized. Paul the apostle could mentor you for three whole years and John could tell you every story of the Person of Christ face-to-face, but if we believe in some small measure that there is still some satisfaction to be had outside of God, that is, His own rule through the wonderful experience of His presence and voice, then the back door is left open to walk out on Him whenever we are tempted with other things. If He has everything, there is nothing left. Jesus said, "the devil...has nothing in Me." There is no handle to grip because all has been handed over to God Himself and His will.

Once I was taken into a vision in which I saw down a long, dark alley a door with a divine light shining out from the bottom and side cracks. I knew heaven was behind this door and I was full of excitement to walk through it. When I tried to enter, it was locked. So I knocked. Out of the top of the door a little slit opened up and I could see eyes looking at me through the door. This man was smiling. I could tell from the look of His eyes that He was happy to see me. I knew it was the Lord.

He said to me, "What is the password?" Immediately I panicked because I had no idea. I thought quickly to myself, Is it a Scripture? A name? A song? I had no idea. I felt helpless and hopeless. I was silent for a long minute. I felt He would shut the slit and I would not be able to come in if I didn't get the password right; I felt that I should have known this. Maybe He told me and I forgot. I was deflated completely. As a grasping effort, hoping to pull on the mercy in His heart, I blurted out, "I only want You, Lord!" Immediately the door was unlocked and the sound of it knocked me out of the vision and I was back in my prayer chair.

This vision taught me so much. It is not knowledge that draws Him to us. It is not the right song or the secret mysteries that mean anything to Him. He is simply looking for that one who only wants Him. That one who finds in Him everything that they could ever desire. As long as other things are looked to we cannot see Him. Let me save you the suspense. Sex, perversions, drugs, a husband or wife, kids, money, a dream job, or even power, miracles, success, a platform, knowledge, or wonders cannot begin to scratch the surface of what it is to have Him as life and pleasure. His presence and person as the satisfaction of our souls is the sweet empowering bliss of life in God and like God.

11

WITHDRAWING WITH GOD

"...the spirit of harlotry is in their midst and they have not known the Lord and the pride of Israel testifies to His face...He has withdrawn Himself from them..." (Hosea 5: 4-6)

MEN BECOME STUBBORN. I HAVE SEEN THIS OVER AND OVER. A literally astounding stubbornness. A resolute and almost fierce adherence to one's own will. Have you gazed into a brother's eyes and seen this before? He who used to love and serve God with the utmost intensity or fervency or maybe even depth of wisdom and understanding has now a stone-cold face against God's living, flowing, experiential voice and presence? I have, and in that very moment it is clear as day that it has a supernatural power involved in it.

The Lord withdraws from harlotry (5:6). If we will not withdraw with Him we will soon withdraw from Him. And since a man has lost the reality of God in his life through other lovers and departing from His presence and voice, he becomes devoted to man's commands. He inevitably trusts in man to deliver him (5:11, 13).

If harlotry continues, God's heart is broken. God has

longed to draw His people to Himself, and as they respond with stubbornness they are broken beyond remedy. There is no remedy for man if he will not come away. Man must acknowledge his guilt and seek His face. And in the case of hard hearts and stubborn souls, God's mercy brings affliction. For affliction has the potential to humble a man and cause him to seek God (5:15).

12

CHRIST TEACHES WHAT HE IS

"Break up your fallow ground, for it is time to seek the Lord until He comes and teaches you righteousness." (Hosea 10:12)

The command to "break up your fallow ground" is connected in this text with "seek the Lord." This teaches us that "hard ground" is a condition of prayerlessness. Where there is no prayer there is no sinking for the seed. The seed literally bounces off. In order for the seed to sink into the ground it must be soft enough to receive it. This is what breaking up fallow ground is. Seeking the Lord is evidence of tilled ground. Seeking the Lord is how the soul is primed and ready for the reception of God's words.

Notice what follows "seek the Lord"—"He comes and teaches you righteousness." The response of Christ to the seeking heart is His presence, "He comes...." The great teacher Himself, in His own presence and from His own mouth, will teach righteousness. Actually there is no other way to learn righteousness. Anyone can teach principles, but Christ teaches what He is. Such teaching causes the words to drop from the brain into the blood. Our problem today, in the words of A.W. Tozer, is that we have "substituted logic for life." Or as Leonard Ravenhill once stated so brilliantly, "We mistake action for unction and commotion for creation."

See, God speaks Himself. Each time God speaks to you He is giving Himself to you. In your maturity as a Christian, you will become exactly what- ever God says to you. He forms you by speaking into you. "He must lead you in the paths of righteousness" for His own name's sake. Becoming righteous unto God is a result of the words of Christ coming into you in His presence, "He comes and teaches you righteousness." Such receptivity of the word into your soul comes from having broken up the fallow ground through putting away all other things and seeking the Lord Himself.

IV

HOW TO PROSPER IN EVERYTHING

13

MATURITY IS ENJOYING GOD

In verse 9 of Genesis 2 the Scripture says that, "the Lord God made to grow." Man is not toiling, sweating, and striving; that is the curse (Genesis 3:19). Man's only job was to enjoy. This may upset people, but the means of stewardship is simply, enjoyment. The way to guard our delight in God is delighting in God.

A dear friend called me one day and asked, "What is one major evidence that a man is maturing in God?" I blurted out without even thinking, "Daily enjoying sweet fellowship with God." Could it be so simple? Yes. God has made it this way. The only thing that can produce godliness in us is Life from God. Life comes by the reception of Him who is Life. We received the Son and in Him have Life. Now we as sons are perpetual recipients of that same Life. This can only come about through the sweet enjoyment of exchange with God.

Back to our original text, the man whose "leaf does not wither" is that man who delights in God. Some may say, "But the Scripture says specifically, that 'his delight is in the law of the Lord,' not the Lord Himself." One quick read through

Psalm 119 will convince us that the law, statutes, instructions, commands, and words of the Lord are all the means by which He is experienced and are themselves indicative of the Lord Himself.

14

THE VISION OF THE LIGHT BEING

DAVID IS NOT HAPPY WITH INK AND LETTERS, BUT THE LIVING God who satisfies the longings of his soul. But somehow, someway, through divine illumination he sees and hears God through the things written. He prays, "Lord, open my eyes to see the wonderful things in Your law." In Psalm 19:7-8 David points to the person of God experienced through the words of God:

"The law of the Lord is perfect, restoring the soul. The testimony of the Lord is sure, making wise the simple. The precepts of the Lord are right, rejoicing the heart. The commandment of the Lord is pure, enlightening the eyes."

In essence he is saying, "I can see it, but I can't see it. There is more than just letters here. God Himself is with me through His words."

A few years back I had a very vivid vision in prayer that will give a picture to the point. I was in a dark room straining to read the Bible. It was fuzzy and very difficult to make out when all of a sudden a Light Being appeared a few feet away, and as I looked up at Him He drew closer and closer. As He did I was able to see clearer and clearer. Without His presence I was blinded, but when I became aware of His presence and turned my attention to His person, He became like a lamp for me to see His words.

What am I trying to say? It is imperative that the Scriptures themselves be cracked open by the weight of His presence. Then His voice can come out of them and into us and the transformation begins. For, "In His Light we see light."

Once we come to the Lord and allow Him to be our satisfaction, which means we have given up on all other things and recognize that only He satisfies, this will inevitably produce in us an endless preoccupation with God Himself. David says, "in His law does he meditate day and night." This is a consuming, a literal obsession with the person of God. We learn from this that meditation is the irruption of delight in God and it reproduces the same. It is like a holy recycling.

15

FEELING GOD

The common question that I receive is, "Why don't I feel God?" And we have all been counseled at one time or another with the state- ment, "We cannot go by what we feel." Is this true? Should we be so indifferent to whether or not we "feel" God that it does not matter either way? Should we be so disconnected from "feeling" His presence that we present experience as some sort of lottery?

Charles Spurgeon once noted, "Only a corpse is without feeling" (The Treasure of David). Philip Krill wrote in his book, Life in the Trinity, "We are never without feeling." John Bunyan wrote of prayer, "Prayer is a sensible feeling in the heart" (Prayer). A. W. Tozer wrote, "...worship not a duty we perform but a presence we experience" (Experiencing the Presence of God). I believe these statements to ring true.

The question is not whether or not we should feel God, but rather what does it mean to "feel God?" The dictionary defines "feeling" as "an emotional state or reaction." Looking into the life of Jesus we see that He did nothing apart from the empowerment of spiritual perception of His Father. Perception is defined as, "the ability to see, or hear or sense."

The sense of God is not just important; it is our source of spiritual empowerment. Our spiritual "feeling" as stated in the Scriptures, is simply, "joy unspeakable and full of glory." First Peter 1:8, "Whom having not seen, ye love; in whom through now ye see him not, yet believing, ye rejoice with joy unspeakable and full of glory."

Yes, this is our portion under His rule. Even though we don't physically see Him, we experience Him, in joy and glory. We don't see Him, but we perceive Him. Moses endured, "seeing Him who is unseen." The early Christian writers spoke of the "imageless vision."

Feeling rightly defined as spiritual perceptibility in the Scriptures simply means that "peace that passes all understanding" is the Life source and guidance of those whose minds and hearts are stayed upon Him.

"And the peace of God, which passes all understanding, shall keep your hearts and minds through Christ Jesus."

Peace enjoyed and beyond comprehension. What does this mean? Well, maybe it could be better seen as this, "It makes absolutely no sense to have peace right now, but I do." Such wonderful peace acts as a guard for your mind and your heart. God's protection over your heart and mind is the experience of His presence that blissfully numbs our souls to doubt, fear, reason, questions, etc. Our only job is to look at Him. Isaiah 26:3:

"You will keep him in perfect peace whose mind is stayed on You."

In the Scriptures, feeling simply means that the rule of the great King established in our souls is not a matter of what we talk about but rather peace and joy in the presence of God who is the Holy Spirit.

> Romans 14:17: *"For the Kingdom of God is not meat and drink; but righteousness, and peace, and joy in the Holy Ghost."*

Rest is the realm of perception and recep- tion of God. God has promised us that when we are under His shadow, joy and peace and comfort and grace and empowerment are not only ours but are our Life supply. Read these next two sentences slowly.

Jesus is the only person who is all at once. The Bliss of His realm is what He in fact is.

When we speak of feelings we are not speaking of physical sensation but rather internal perceptibility. Yet, at the same time Thomas Dubay once wrote, "We are so one that the interinfluence between spiritual and material elements is unavoidable" (Fire Within). There are many times that our bodies experience the overflow of the glorious inflow of God. David writes in Psalm 23 that his cup was so full to the brim that it overflowed to the outside of the cup. The external feelings are not what is promised. What is promised to us is the experience of God's person when we come to Him. Rest itself is a promised feeling and work of the Lamb of God who said in Matthew 11:28,

> *"Come to me and I will give you rest."*

Satisfaction is itself a promised feeling. Jesus said in John 7:37, "...if any man is thirsty let him come to Me and drink."

Being fed in our spirit is a feeling we can feel, and Jesus said that He would feed those who hunger (see John 6).

Feeling is inseparable from experience. Experience is inseparable from feeling. People ask me if I experience God every time that I pray. My answer is always the same. Yes, because without experience it is simply not communion with a person.

A. W. Tozer once wrote, "The tragedy of the church is that from childhood to old age men have only known a synthetic God compounded of theology and logic; having no eyes to see and no ears to hear" (Evenings With Tozer). The terrible indictment against the church is that we have substituted logic for Life. Jesus condemned the Pharisees not because of their lack of knowing God's words but because they had no idea what God was saying and no living experience of God's person.

Feeling God, experiencing God, is not an option or perk of His presence. It is rather the means by which He frees us and empowers us to be able to obey Him. The experience of God is the enjoyment of the New Covenant, the Covenant in which God Himself would make His abode in us. John 14:23:

"If a man love me, he will keep my words; and my Father will love him, and we will come unto him, and make our abode with him."

The Covenant in which God would put His Spirit on the inside of us. First Corinthians 2:12:

"We have received...the Spirit which is of God."

The Covenant that is spoken of as new wine. The Covenant in which our fellowship is with Jesus Christ the Son. The Covenant in which seeing and hearing, experiencing, and yes, even sensing the Glorious Word of Life within is our lot, our source, and our strength. Jesus refused to act outside of the empowerment of spiritually perceiving His Father, saying, "The Son can do nothing of Himself. He can only do what He sees His Father doing...." Because He is the Son and the only prototype man, He reveals to us that a son can do nothing of himself. This is the reason why religion hates sonship. Jesus was calling God His own Father and they had not been born of God.

None of Jesus' works had their origin in Himself, but all of their works issued out of themselves. Jesus is showing us that sonship has its roots in the great love with which the Father has loved us in giving to us His own Spirit, and that walking out sonship is living in synchronization with God through spiritual perception of God.

V

UNION

16

BECOMING TRUE

St. Patrick of Ireland wrote, "...*the lying mouth kills the soul. The same Lord has said in the gospel, 'on that day of judgment men will have to give an explanation for every idle word which they have spoken' (Matthew 12:36). Therefore, I ought to worry exceedingly with fear and trembling the sentence for that day when none can escape or hide and all will have to give an account of the smallest sins before the judgment seat of Christ.*"
—(St. Patrick: His Confessions and Other Works [Catholic Book Publishing Corp., 2009], 13)

AFTER THAT STRIKING ACCOUNT FROM ST. PATRICK'S confessions, I was alone in silence for afternoon prayer in a church called St. Peter and Paul on the fifteenth day of March, and as the presence of God came heavily upon me, I was in an instant extremely convicted of the lies I have implied by remaining silent, or lies of embellishments in storytelling, or exaggerations for excitement's sake, or simply not telling the whole truth. So I reached out to the Lord for forgiveness, and as I did I was granted humility for repentance. When I was repenting I had a confirmation of the

Spirit by gold dust on my left hand. I felt in my heart to check the date. I remembered it was March 15. As I thought of what the significance could be, the Holy Spirit reminded me of 1 Timothy 3:15, *"...I tarry long, that thou mayest know how thou oughtest to behave thyself in the house of God, which is the church of the living God, the pillar and ground of the truth"* (KJV).

The church is the *"pillar and ground of TRUTH."* We must be true. Jesus is the Truth. The Spirit is called the Spirit of Truth. I remember Art Katz saying, *"Men seek truths, but God seeks to make us true. The truth is the whole truth and nothing but the truth or it is not the truth at all."* So I pray along with St. Alphonsus Ligouri, *"... nail my heart to Your feet, that it may ever remain there, to love You, and never leave You again. I love You more than myself; I repent of having offended You. Grant that I may love You always; and then do with me whatever You will."*

We must always remember that apart from Him, we are fountains of wickedness. And that if we leave His embrace our face will turn against Him. Abiding is not just a good idea; if we don't abide we will end up being burned. However you want to look at that, be it hell, outer darkness, destruction of a life ... regardless, it is not a good thing and is a harsh image spoken from the mouth of the Christ for a reason. His embrace is where He speaks. His embrace is what makes us like Him.

17

LET HIM HOLD YOU

I was watching Fulton Sheen the other day on YouTube. He quoted two statistics that I thought were particularly interesting concerning touch in the human life. Two rooms were full of babies that needed care. In the first room, each of the babies was cared for by individual mothers. In the second room, each of the babies was cared for by one nurse. Thirty-nine percent of the children in the second room died and all the children in the first room lived. Is there significant correlation between life and touch? In the spiritual counterpart, could it be that the lifelessness, for a vast part of the church today, is due to a lack of touch? Not human touch, but the touch of God. Is there death in the church because we have failed to point people to the touch of God's hand or the embrace of His arms? Have our theological views relegated God's embrace of the human soul to a symbol?

Could it be that a large part of our deep depravity in prayer is due to a lack of our souls receiving the embrace of God?

The second particularly interesting statistic was that

babies who have very little touch in their lives take longer to learn how to walk and speak. Again, in the spiritual counterpart, could it be that many Christians have a very difficult time maturing by reason of a lack of touch? Could it be that a large part of our deep depravity in prayer is due to a lack of our souls receiving the embrace of God?

The analogy is imperfect because God is not responsible for the lack of embrace. The fault falls on our unwillingness to fall into His arms. My personal belief is that without the embrace of God in our lives, we are quickly decaying. When I say, "touch of God" I mean His sweet embrace. I mean His holding. I mean His genuine tight clinching of our souls into His warm and tender chest. I mean, finding in Him our only refuge from life's pressures.

The other day I saw my daughter crying in her room about something. I was deeply concerned, so I walked into the room and bent down to her level and sweetly asked her, "What is wrong, baby?" She began to tell me her pressing issue. She expounded on her disturbing problem and I picked her up and laid her head on my chest and I said, "Whenever you feel frustrated, sad, angry, confused or hurt or anything…you run straight to Daddy and I'll put your head on my chest and you can find rest. Forget about everything else and just know that I am here. I can help you. After you calm down. I can handle whatever it is." She didn't respond with anything but a deep sigh of comfort and quietness as she rested on my chest and I rubbed her back. In that moment, though there were no words going back and forth, we were communicating. I believe we were communicating higher than words. I believe we were exchanging. There was a transferring of my rest into her problem.

Brothers and sisters, the embrace of God is so important. Can you hear Him saying that to you? Can you see His beckoning hand? Can you imagine His open arms? Allow the Spirit of God to woo you away from your sins, failures, weaknesses, performance, strivings, issues, troubles, and trials, into His arms. This is simultaneously the mark of maturity and the maturing work; how well we remain in His embrace.

18

IF YOU SEEK ME FOR POWER...

...YOU WILL FORFEIT INTIMACY...

ONE OF THE FIRST KEYS TO EXPERIENCING INTIMACY WITH JESUS is the understanding that He is the man in the relationship and we are the women. We receive. The bride didn't say, "I am going to kiss him with the kisses of my mouth," but rather, "Let Him kiss me...." Yielding is the secret; the ceasing of efforts and our still surrender in adoration. Everything aside, He just wants your heart (mind, will, and emotions). When we come to Him, we do not come to intercede for others or gain answers to prayer or fulfill a religious duty. We don't come to Him to manipulate Him into doing something for us. We do not even come to Him because we need to. Though we do need to, it is not the motive.

Once God spoke to my heart and said, "If you seek Me for power, you will forfeit intimacy." We come simply because there is no greater lover or pleasure in the entire world and this is the reason why we were created by God—to live in God. We simply come to Him because we just want to be with Him. Only He is lovely, wonderful, and true. He is truly holy, meaning altogether separate and other than anything else. We must have a genuine desire to want to be with Him.

Without this, or if this is trumped by anything else, no matter how noble or legitimate, we are bankrupt. Please catch this. We come to Him for no other reason than Him. Do you love His presence? Do you love His voice? In Mark chapter 3, His presence and voice were exactly what Jesus set the disciples aside for, "To be with Him."

19

CHIEF LUMINARY

The paramount issue and direct medication to cure both the oppression upon God's people's lives and the rebellion in God's people's hearts is and will always be God's Radiant Face.

Oh, the Chief Luminary! God has installed in creation an undeviating parallel to the brilliance of His countenance. The splendor of the suspended luminous sun shining from the firmament pictures for us the Resplendent Son of God shining in our hearts. It is a supportive analogy, yet as all types do, it falls short to communicate the whole, though we can hold it high enough to see through it a vision of God and His supernatural nature. No man has seen God, for He dwells in light that cannot be approached, the brightness of which is His very own person. For God is Light. In His mercy, and by His humble choosing, He has exactly represented Himself in the shining face of Jesus Christ, the crucified and risen God-man.

A right understanding of what is meant by the word "face" is imperative. For in the "face of Jesus" is the revelation of God. And within this prayer is a parallel between the sun that lights the earth's mountains, rivers, and fields, and the face of the Son who illuminates the soul by His Spirit. Without the sun the earth would be swallowed by darkness. Light is defined as, "that upon which all colors depend," simply because without its illuminative function, sight is inhibited. So it is with all things upon the earth and the earth itself. The sun is our illumination, the agent of sight in our world. The parallel is at no other point truer. Without Jesus, who is the "light of the world," there exists no vision, no understanding, no clarity, for darkness reigns with its fatal companions of confusion, doubt, death, and sin...

The glory of God is the shining countenance of God in the face of Christ, radiant with the splendor of the Spirit. Our restoration is unto the luminous brilliance of interactive fellowship with the Godhead. He is the triumphant bliss, joy, and pleasure of life. The heat of the sun illuminates the barren earth into fertility, and God's Son shines down with the restoration and salvation of His countenance, illuminating the human soul, passing it into Godlikeness. God is light. He passes through the unobstructed soul into the affairs of men...

I recently heard a story of a little Catholic girl who loved to turn her attention every Sunday to the massive stained glass windows of the saints in the cathedral during her Sunday school classes. The instructor one day submitted a question to the young group of Catholic pupils. She asked, "Does anyone know what a saint is?" All the children began to look around at each other without a clue as to what a saint actually is. Then the little admirer of the stained glass windows very simply stated, while staring right into a stained glass icon of St. Francis, "They are the ones that the sun shines through." Though the answer was so simple, even too simple, the simplicity of such an answer was the golden truth.

It was the simplistic articulation and imagery of God's unification with man; we are those through whom the light of the Son of God shines. God is light, and if we live in the light of unobstructed fellowship with Him, He will shine through us in sweet union of Spirit, fellowship, and life.

VI

INTO THE CLOUD

20

ONE THING IS NECESSARY

WHAT MANY PEOPLE DO NOT UNDERSTAND IS THAT THE SOUL was made to do all things while looking at Jesus, so that everything done—whether eating or drinking, cleaning or working, preaching or praying, teaching or counseling—is done unto the glory of God. But God only receives glory when our works issue from a continuous state of adoration and fixation upon Him. While Martha's actions issued from what she was doing, Mary's legacy was rooted in who she was.

Jesus coins the phrase tattooed on the heart of every lovesick believer: "only one thing is necessary." Jesus frankly states that His presence and voice are the only essential things. Martha's labors were unneeded, unnecessary, and pointless, simply because they were from a different realm.

Naturally they were significant, for who wouldn't serve Jesus if He came to their house? It is in a woman's nature to serve. Even Peter's mother-in-law waited on Jesus as soon as He raised her up from her sickbed. But, even though the natural mind sees this service as significant, God calls us into a higher realm specifically to conform us to His image of His

Son through the receiving of His life by His presence and voice. He is after an experiential union that only comes through an experiential fellowship.

We must realize that the realm of human service has never pleased God, because only God pleases God. Witness Lee said, "Even if you could submit to God on your own, it wouldn't please God, because God is only pleased with His Son." The only thing that pleases God is what He does Himself.

Mary is in the becoming realm where contemplation and activity are united in being. That is what God is after: men who become the message, who plunge themselves into Him and become like Him. Sons of God will say with Jesus, "I can do nothing on My own," and will live as Jesus, "My Father abiding in Me does His works."

The choice is yours.

Jesus says, "Mary has chosen." The tragedy about this picture is the equally available Christ and our freedom to not choose Him. Martha preferred what made sense to her, what was naturally and outwardly acceptable as service. In direct contrast, Mary chose "the good part": His presence, His face, and His voice, by drawing near, bowing low, and gazing attentively upon Him.

I tell you that the good fruit from the good tree comes from choosing the good part, which is eating from the hand of the Good Shepherd. This life is as indestructible as God, for Jesus says it "shall not be taken away from her." Because this reception of God is of true eternal significance, it cannot be lost.

Maybe this concept of being in God's presence is foreign to you. My heart breaks for those who have only known adherence to rules and restrictions, service and duty. God never had that kind of life in mind. He sent His own Son to the earth in order to bring the relation- ship He has with the

Son to us. He endured separation from the Son to reconcile man to Himself and restore blissful union with us.

Those who have received His Spirit are His very own family. There is no analogy that can sufficiently convey what His life is like, for it is in a category all by itself. But I promise that if you will lay your life down to live dependently upon His presence, you will receive a constant flow of life on the inside that works in you both to will and do for His good pleasure.

Art Katz once said, "Sonship is when you cannot tell where the one begins and the other ends." Jesus refused to do anything outside of spiritually perceiving God's desires. We must recognize that apart from Him we are impotent; but when we choose to do only what He is doing, He causes His own works to be ours.

21

SEPARATION

"Jesus took with Him Peter and James and John his brother, and led them up on a high mountain by themselves."

THE FOUNDATION OF YOUR LIFE IN HIM IN PUBLIC IS RECEIVING life from Him in private. First, Christ separated these specific individuals from the rest. The first secret to a life focused upon Jesus is seasons of separation from the world and others to be alone with Him. It is imperative to get away with Him.

Why is this so important if we live in perpetual fellowship with Him throughout the day? The simple answer is because the secret place is the power of the abiding place; the foundation of your life in Him in public is receiving life from Him in private.

I don't mean to make anyone uncomfortable, but the truth is that just as there are certain things a husband and wife will do only when they're alone together, there are certain things Jesus will only do with you when you are alone with Him.

When Jesus taught on prayer in the sixth chapter of Matthew, He said, "...go into your closet...." This is separation. Leave the company of others and get alone. Then He said, "...shut the door...." He not only wants us to separate ourselves, but He also wants us to shut out the noise.

Separation, solitude, and silence are the siblings of prayer. As Art Katz, a mighty spokesman of God, once said, you must "...be ruthless with yourself to get alone, lock the door and seek God and be found by Him."

In John 3:22, the Scripture says, "After these things Jesus and His disciples went into the land of Judea and there He was spending time with them..."

Here are three elements of Christ's discipleship:

1. Without time there can be no discipleship. The number one seed sown into your life to yield forth an increase is time. Time is our spiritual fermentation.
2. What kind of time? It is time with Him, being in the presence of Jesus, which will miraculously fashion us into true followers of Jesus. Andrew Murray said, "Christ's presence was the training of the disciples."

When you "spend time with someone," it is not a matter of simply sitting with them, but rather communicating and exchanging with that individual. When we spend time with Jesus, His voice and presence disciple and guide us.

Thomas Merton wrote, "Without solitude of some sort, there is and can be no maturity." He continues: "There must be a time of day when the man who makes plans forgets his plans, and acts as if he had no plans at all. There must be a time of day when the man who has to speak falls very silent.

And his mind forms no more propositions.... There must be a time when the man of resolutions puts aside his resolutions as if they had all been broken.

22

DIRECT CONTACT

"He came to them." It is crucial to understand that Jesus responds to the disciples' humility by drawing even nearer. Not only do they see the glory of the Son and hear the voice of the Father, but as they cast themselves to the earth in humble adoration, they are approached by the Son.

Jesus touches them. Direct contact through the revelation of the Son in the presence of God is the most transformative work there is. Jacob's whole walk was changed after a touch on the hip; the dead boy being carried out of the city in a coffin was raised by one touch of His hand; multitudes were healed by simply receiving His touch. The hand of Christ is the channel through which the electric current of God's very person flows.

For these disciples, the specific result of having been touched by Him was this: "When they lifted up their eyes they saw nothing else but Jesus alone." The secret to a sustained vision of Jesus is direct contact with God, and the secret to direct contact with God is a sustained vision of Jesus.

It is interesting to note that the three men who shared this encounter were three distinctly different individuals whose callings were vastly different. I believe they point to three specific kinds of believers that an exchange with Christ produces.

First, James was one of the earliest martyrs of the church, representing the spirit of martyrdom. Direct contact with God will produce people who are willing to lay their heads upon the block for Christ, fearless before the spirit of the world.

Second, Peter's shadow healed the sick; I believe he represents carrying the glory of God. Direct contact with Christ will produce carriers of God's glory. As Bill Johnson said, "Your shadow will release whatever over- shadows you."

Lastly, John is the beloved disciple. Direct contact with God will produce lovesick revelators who can access the divine Person and rest their heads upon His breast.

This kind of bridal union and contact with Jesus is articulated so well by Mother Basilea Schlink:

"I come to live within you." Our Lord and Savior Jesus says this to every Christian soul. Prepare for me a lodging with ardent love and longing, that I may with your soul unite. Prepare your hearts chamber, put far all earthly Clamor, silence all worldly longings now. Upon you take my quietness, eternities own stillness, and my approaching footsteps here. Give up your will entirely, surrender all completely to me, and to my will be given. Then can I make my dwelling, within your heart now reigning, one then with you and love and pain. What then could be more glorious or sweeter than your presence within my heart, oh Jesus Christ? Now all with any silence that you may come to enter myself and make it yours.

"He will live only in hearts that love Him. Only there does He desire to dwell. Loving Him means giving Him first place. It means nothing can stir our hearts as He does.

"We need to be on our guard against being overwhelmed

by earth's joys and sorrows, by our work and activities. When such things preoccupy us, Jesus no longer has first place in our lives and has to leave the innermost chamber of our heart. Nothing that concerns, excites, or upsets us should be allowed to penetrate into that sanctuary where He lives and has His throne. Ultimately, nothing should disquiet us, because He who is our peace is living in the deepest recesses of our heart.

For bridal souls, there is no greater fear than losing their first love by being absorbed with the joys and troubles and the ups and downs of daily life. He requires of us total devotion: He will not share the throne of our hearts with anyone or anything else. He will not have us dominated by troubles, cares, people, or the things of this world. This is why a bridal soul wholeheartedly resists all such influences that might take control of her. He alone is to reign in her. His indwelling is her greatest joy and happiness. All this means she has a deep inner peace regardless of any external pressures and troubles weighing upon her. She is always one with Him, He and her and she and Him."

23

ABRAHAM: FRIENDSHIP WITH GOD

God identified Himself as the God of Abraham. Though Abraham was not perfect, God's deep relation- ship with him reveals the fact that He chooses to identify Himself with flawed people, simply because they believe, love, and obey Him. It is evident that He chooses to identify Himself with flawed people, simply because they believe, love, and obey Him.

Abraham's fellowship with God brought him to an incredibly intimate bond with God—he is the only man singled out in his day.

This mutually affectionate relationship was a bond of covenant friends. Think of how deep this bond went, where God questioned whether or not He should keep a secret from Abraham. Did you catch that? God actually thought to Himself, "Should I hide what I am about to do from Abraham?" God didn't share with Abraham what was coming just because He could, but because He desired to.

God's communion with Abraham was at such an intimate place that God unfolded His own future plans in no uncertain terms; Abraham was told exactly what God was going to do: where, when, why, how. And here is the most amazing part—this information was actually an invitation to intercede, an opportunity to co-labor with God.

Many of us love to think that our own relationship with God is at this level of intimacy, but so few of us have actually ever been divinely shown specific future events and invited to pray through them. Do you know God like this? Is this intimacy a reality in your life? Does God desire to open His blueprints before your eyes, giving you specific details to carry out?

I am not just referring to unveiling the mysteries revealed in the Scriptures concerning His plan for the ages, but also His present work in your own family, friends, church, city, and nation. This, my friend, is the definition of a covenant friend of God: someone who has God's trust. Trusting in the Lord begins this relationship; your trust in God should lead you into faithfulness to God where He can trust you.

Jesus said to the disciples, "I call you friends." These are those whom He knew had already left everything to follow Him and would eventually give their lives in faithfulness to Him. Just like Abraham, they were those with whom the Lord found it desirable and necessary to share His specifics. Can you imagine God saying to Himself, "Shall I hide from [insert your name] what I am going to do?

For example, perhaps a family member of yours has rebelled against God and is partying with other nonbelievers, and while you commune with God, He shares with you that the whole party is going to go up in smoke. When you recognize that information as an invitation to intercede, you begin to pray mercy and salvation for your loved one. Later you find out that a disaster did occur at the party, but a good Christian friend who felt uneasy about being there took your sister or brother away just before the catastrophe.

God does many things in the earth this way, inviting us to

take part in bringing the Kingdom of heaven to earth. This is why He cherishes His friends: simply because they listen to Him, because they commune with Him, and because He can trust them. Doesn't this kind of relationship sound desirable to you?

Maybe you already live in this place. Praise God! But, I submit to you that there is always more in His heart for those who are willing to plunge into it. If you haven't experienced this, do you want to? If you have, do you want more? How do we reach this place of friendship and trust?

24

MOSES, AARON, AND SAMUEL

The other day I was on my way to an early morning prayer meeting, passing through the city at about 5:00 a.m. The clouds were so low that at a particular section of the highway I entered the fog. When I was in this cloud, I could only see what was directly in front of me, illuminated by the beam of my headlights.

If I had not seen the city before I entered the cloud, there would have been no way to know that I was even in the city. It didn't matter how high the buildings were or how many of them there were—I was blinded to their existence by the cloud. Of course, this did not mean that the buildings were no longer there, but they were invisible to me while I drove through the cloud.

This is a great parallel of the life we can live in the presence of the Spirit. When we enter His presence (the cloud), we are blinded to the multiple massive earthly structures towering over us. In the cloud we are shrouded with Him and cannot see the cares of the world, the oppression of the authorities, the monetary system, the lusts of this life, the strivings of human nature; all is swallowed by the cloud.

The psalmist mentions three men in particular who chose to go into the cloud. They not only saw this cloud, as did the rest of the children of Israel, but actually entered into it. They gave themselves to the presence of God, casting all that they were, both positive and negative, into the cloud.

Please do not read these next four words lightly: THEY CHOSE TO ENTER. Have you chosen to enter? It means leaving all other things behind in order to experience Him. This is the decision we must make: we must lay all other things aside or we won't be allowed to go inside.

The cloud is the manifestation of God's very person, His glory, His presence, and these men entered into it!

Moses, the most humble man upon the earth. Numbers 12:3, "Now the man Moses was very humble, more than any man who was on the face of the earth."

Aaron, "the spokesman." Exodus 7:1-2, "Aaron shall be your prophet. You shall speak all that I command you, and your brother Aaron shall speak to Pharaoh...."

Samuel, the one who never had a word fall to the ground. First Samuel 3:19, "Thus Samuel grew and the Lord was with him and let none of his words fail."

MOSES

I wish to call your attention to the order in which these men are mentioned. Is it any wonder why Moses comes first? Humility is the foundation of all things erected by God, the vacuum by which we receive grace, the very image of God in man! To what else does God lend His merciful hand? In what other disposition doesGod chose to dwell?

Humility is both rudimentary and paramount; without it there is no commencement of divine activity. The Cure d'Ars, a miracle-working lover of Jesus from 1800s France, wrote,

"Without humility man only has the appearance of virtues." I am thoroughly convinced that God prefers an ounce of humility to a ton of talent and gifts.

AARON

Aaron, the spokesman, is connected to the humility that Moses represents. Through this we see that the speaking of Aaron must walk side by side with Moses' humility. Speaking for God and humility are inseparably related—humility is the brother of the oracles of God. There is no spokesman who can stand without humility, for everything he says comes from humility.

A spokesman that does not come from humility does not originate from God. Humility enters the cloud and the spokesman speaks what he received from the cloud. Moses went into the cloud to directly hear God's heart. Aaron entered the cloud to receive the message he would later deliver.

If a spokesman tries to enter the cloud without being led by humility, he will not hear what he is to say because the oracle comes to humility for the spokesman to deliver. Aaron's job was to communicate what God installed in Moses, and his powerful speaking came from Moses' humble hearing.

We must speak the things that God has said. As His spokesman in the earth, we are the voice of the Most High in the world. Entering into the presence of God with humility is the origin of all our declaration. We enter the presence in humility and hear what we are to carry to God's people and the world.

When John the Baptist was asked who he was, he said "I am a voice...," claiming no identity in himself. He was not selfishly invested in his own existence at all, but was consumed by hearing, proclaiming, and preparing for God's Word. Like John, the spokesman completely gives himself over to listening, always mindful that everything he is depends upon hearing God.

SAMUEL

Samuel represents the last stage of those who enter the cloud. Samuel's words took on the unfailing quality of God's words simply because he only spoke God's pure words. As Madame Guyon wrote in her commentary on Exodus, "It is the property of God's speaking to absorb our own." Those who go into the cloud can be assured that not one of their words will fall to the ground simply because they are of 100 percent divine origin.

Samuel was unique among all the other prophets before and after him because he was both a priest and a prophet. He may be the only one of his kind, both ministering directly to the Lord in the Tabernacle unashamedly speaking God's Word and executing God's will in public.

Hebrews 11:32 states concerning Samuel: "Samuel and the prophets." A modern comparison could be, "Jordan and the Bulls." Some have explained this passage saying, "Samuel was not exclusively a prophet." Samuel is singled out. Regardless of whether this is because he was a prophet among prophets or because he had both priestly and prophetic duties, he was an exceptional servant of God.

He was not afraid to wield the sword and execute what others were religiously and politically afraid to. Nor did he ever allow for partial obedience, severing himself from all allegiance to the world and its rulers. Samuel was ruthlessly and unyieldingly obedient to God.

OBEDIENCE

THE HUMILITY of Moses received the Word, the mouth of Aaron spoke the Word, and Samuel executed the Word. These three kept the testimonies of the Lord and obeyed Him, painting a picture of the obedient life that results from entering and carrying the glory cloud.

Some may disagree with this statement, but I believe that obedience to God is only possible when God emanates out of a man. When a man lays his life aside to enter into the presence of God and hear His voice, his own soul will be empowered with delight to do God's will.

Jesus, the Word of God Himself, "delighted to do God's will." Hearing the Word of God gives delight for obeying the will of God. Power to fulfill God's will is found in receiving the Word of God itself.

What is so unique about these men? They are distinguished by the fact that when God invited them into the cloud, they entered in. They were swallowed by the cloud when they heard Him speak. This could be our distinction as well. If you are looking to hear God's sweet voice, it is most clearly heard in His sweet presence. Enter into His presence and stay there, saturated and soaked, perfumed and permeated with His person. John 1:1 says, "In the beginning was the Word and the Word was with God and the Word was God." Notice that the Word was "with God." The Word is in God's presence. Remember in Exodus 34 the reason why Moses' face shone: a shining face is connected with receiving God's voice.

Another result of entering the cloud is that they were heard or answered by the Lord. First John says, "And if we know that He hears us in whatever we ask, we know that we have the requests which we have asked from Him."

John also records Jesus telling us that when we abide in Him, we receive answers to prayer. "If you abide in Me, and My words abide in you, ask whatever you wish, and it will be done for you." God answers the life that abides and lingers in the cloud of His presence.

25

THE KEY TO UNLOCKING AMERICA

ONE TIME, WHILE REINHARD BONNKE WAS PREACHING ABOUT the key that opened Africa to the Gospel, I asked the Lord about what key would unlock America.

I felt deep in my heart that the key to awakening America is wine, namely, the experience of the Spirit. If this is true, the glory of the Lord will only manifest when a servant abandons his life so completely to the specific speaking of God that he obeys God in whatever He wishes.

Jesus said, "Glorify Me that I might glorify you." God invested His glory into the Son, and through His obedience, the Son returned that glory back to the Father through utterly abandoning Himself to God's will. Jesus prayed, "...not My will, but Yours be done." There is no glory to God in a life lived for itself. The prerequisite for giving glory to God is to give ourselves completely to Him. "Whatsoever He saith unto you, do it."

26

AM I NOT WORTH MORE TO YOU THAN 10 SONS?

"Am I not more to you than ten sons?" (1 Samuel 1:8)

"Now there was a certain man from Ramathaim-zophim from the hill country of Ephraim, and his name was Elkanah...He had two wives: the name of one was Hannah and the name of the other Peninnah; and Peninnah had children, but Hannah had no children. Now this man would go up from his city yearly to worship and to sacrifice to the Lord of hosts in Shiloh... When the day came that Elkanah sacrificed, he would give portions to Peninnah his wife and to all her sons and her daughters; but to Hannah he would give a double portion, for he loved Hannah, but the Lord had closed her womb. Her rival, however, would provoke her bitterly to irritate her, because the Lord had closed her womb. It happened year after year, as often as she went up to the house of the Lord, she would provoke her; so she wept and would not eat. Then Elkanah her husband said to her, "Hannah, why do you weep and why do you not eat and why is your heart sad? Am I not better to you than ten sons?" Then Hannah rose after eating and drinking in Shiloh. Now Eli the priest was sitting on the seat by the doorpost of the temple of the Lord. She, greatly distressed, prayed to the Lord and wept bitterly. She made a vow and said, "O Lord of hosts, if You will indeed look on the affliction of Your maidservant and remember me, and not forget Your maidservant, but will give Your maidservant a son, then I will give him to the Lord all the days of his life, and a razor shall never come on his head." (1 Samuel 1:1-11)

In the day and culture in which Elkanah and Hannah lived, a woman found her identity and dignity in bearing children. Her main role was to give her husband children, especially a son to carry on the father's name and line. The fruitfulness of her womb was the culture's only measure of success and value for a woman.

Elkanah's other wife, Peninnah, had a fruitful womb. Her "production" testified to her culture that she was a successful wife, and her "productivity" was her confidence. Having many children awarded her dignity, identity, and praise, removing the pressure of the culture's thought patterns off of her shoulders. Her fruitfulness gave evidence as a prideful witness that she had proven herself in accordance with her culture.

Hannah, on the other hand, though she was greatly loved, was barren and had the pressure of the culture constantly weighing down on her. Obviously, the provocative testimony of the other wife was internally vexing, degrading, and humiliating. Hannah suffered such emotional pressure and humiliation that she was sick to her stomach and could not eat.

The mind-set of the culture demanded that she produce something that she was simply unable to. This constant tension broke her soul. She was distraught and oppressed by the cultural traditions, but most of all, Hannah was shamed by Peninnah's fruitful life.

Peninnah provoked her, but the power she had over Hannah did not come from Peninnah herself, but rather from the patterns of thinking in their culture. Ultimately, Hannah was oppressed by the voice of human demand, human systems, and human traditions.

Do you relate to Hannah? Are you depressed and frustrated with your ministry, judging its success by the numbers (of salvations, of healings, of responses) or results? Are you burdened because your ministry is not growing or frustrated because the unsaved haven't submitted to the Gospel through your witness? If there is any competition hidden in your veins, or any jealousy harbored in your soul, keep reading. I promise that Jesus will eradicate it through one phrase.

When Hannah comes to her husband, he gives the greatest portrayal of the heart of Jesus Christ that there could be in this situation by saying, "Am I not more to you than ten sons?" It is almost as if he was hurt by the fact that something else was the measure of her life.

These words reveal to us that, in his great love for her, he looked for the reason why she was not fulfilled by his love alone. He asks her, "Am I not of more value to you than many children?" Ten is a great number because it represents completion, and as stated earlier, Sons are the greatest fruit a woman can have. Elkanah is asking his oppressed wife in her frustration, "Am I not more to you than all the fruit in the world?"

My dear friend, this is the heart of Jesus. In the same way, He asks: "Are you not fulfilled in Me? Am I not enough? Am I not all sufficient? Am I not I AM? Is fruit (results) more precious to you than I am? Why do you need something more than Me to be happy, satisfied, or delighted? My heart hurts because you are not fulfilled by My love."

I believe some of our frustrated prayers break God's heart, for they reveal to Him that He is no longer the center of our hearts. Jesus' heart is broken by much of our ambition for results, for it replaces Him as the source and joy of life. To be loved by you is the goal of His loving you.

Elkanah gives Hannah such a shocking love that exists outside the thought processes of man. His love finds value in her without demanding fruitfulness as the culture does; his love wants her to be satisfied only with him; in his love, the couple needs nothing more than each other.

In response to such a loving statement from her husband that proved he only wanted her for herself, she stopped weeping, got up, found her appetite, and communed with her husband at the table. The sad fact is that much of our crying for fruit has robbed us of sweet communion with Jesus. And though in the next verse she again cries for fruitfulness, her tears are different; we find a subtle change that makes all the difference in the entire world.

She still pleads for a son, the best fruit, but now it is for a totally different reason. Her motive is changed and purified. While her first cries came from the painful weight of the system of man that wrapped her identity and dignity in productivity and fruitfulness, her last cry is simply to have fruit to be able to give to God. She wants to bear the best fruit to be able to offer at the feet of God Himself.

She is no longer bound by thinking of her own face and testifying of her own life in accordance with the system of the culture, speaking man's language of success, beating herself for lack of fruit, and comparing her life to others.

Now she is free to find all her joy in her husband and not worry if he will leave her if she is unable to produce. Now she cries to God for the right reason, lifting up her tears in purity and weeping out of selflessness. She no longer wants fruit to validate herself; she wants fruit to present to God, to give something of value to Him instead of seeking to be valued by her culture.

One may say, "The Scripture stated earlier that God had closed her womb, so her fruitlessness was because of God." Exactly! Sometimes God prevents us from bearing the fruit that we want so that He can look into our eyes and say, "Am I not more to you than ten sons?"

When God spoke this to me personally, He broke me out of a bondage that I didn't even know I was in, breaking me into a realm of freedom, rest, and ease beyond anything I could have ever thought possible; a realm where the literal joy of heaven and the wine of the Spirit could be consumed for the right reason—intimate union.

A preacher who is looking for more signs and wonders; a pastor who wants a building; an evangelist who desires to see more numbers; a teacher who wants more committed students—whatever your frustration for productivity might be, in your frustration listen to the heart of your Bridegroom, for it beats this lovely phrase, "Am I not more to you than those things? Am I not enough for you? Am I not more to you than a building? Am I not more to you than miracles? Am I not more to you than souls being saved? Am I not more to you than apparent fruitfulness?"

This issue must be settled first: If we are ever to pray with a pure cry, we must be satisfied with Him alone. If we ever want to be pure enough to simply desire to lay fruit at His feet, we must find such contentment with His simple love and presence, forsaking the longings for our own significance.

This issue of being satisfied with God alone will open up our hearts to offer to Jesus our substance. Hannah says, "I will give him to You all the days of his life." Her heart cries, "This fruit is not for my name; no one will even see me with him. This fruit is not to remove my disgrace and shame or to give me dignity or identity...it is all for You, and You alone."

We will be forever set free from the oppressive demand for production when we settle in our hearts that Jesus alone in our lives in daily experience is enough to satisfy everything that we could ever desire. He is enough!

Brothers and sisters, we must return to first love— love that is solely set upon Him alone and satisfied with Him alone, so that fruit can be exactly what it is supposed to be— the work of God, performed by God and offered to God for God alone.

May we never fall into the trap of finding our identity and dignity in how much we have done and can do for the Lord, or how much God has used us, because the real issue is this: if He Himself is not enough, your fruit will be tainted because it was not conceived out of the purity of satisfaction with God alone—you will never birth a Samuel into the world. Peninnah's children were just regular kids that you never hear anything else about; their names, lives, and works perished with them. But Samuel was set apart— he was a loyal prophet and burning priest unlike any other; his words never fell to the ground; there is no other prophet-priest like Samuel except for Jesus Himself. His life is a picture of enduring supernatural work and an exposition of the everlasting effects that will accompany the life satisfied with God alone; he represents the eternal impact of a life in love with the Bridegroom.

In Hebrews the author writes, "...Samuel and the prophets...," indicating that Samuel was significant in all the records of time. He stood out from those who stood out and shone above those who shone.

Significant fruit like Samuel is born only after the question is settled and we can say with all our hearts, "You, Yourself are more to me than all the fruit and success in the world. If I have everything and I don't have You, I have nothing; but If I have You and nothing else in the world, I have everything." Join me in praying: "Jesus, You are more than enough for me, and my desire for fruit is only to have an offering to lay at Your feet."

27

A CAUTION ON IDENTITY

BROTHERS, I AM AFRAID THAT WE ARE IN DANGER OF ECLIPSING our dependency upon the experiential, abiding fellowship in Jesus with the truth concerning our identity in Him. It seems we have become so taken with what He has made us that we no longer recognize our desperate need of Him, not only in our teaching but also in our daily lives. I can hear Keith Green's timeless voice singing, "It's so hard to see when my eyes are on me." Is it possible that by looking so intently at who we are in Him, we have shifted our gaze from Him?

How do we endure in this life? Is it by looking at ourselves or by looking to Jesus? Richard Wurmbrand once said, "The 'I' must be abolished. 'I no longer live,' not the old Paul, not the new Paul, but Christ lives in me." In fact, the anthem of the new nature should be, "Worthy is the Lamb."

Our identity in Christ is wrapped up in looking at Jesus in worship, depending upon Jesus, and receiving from Him our daily bread, waiting and abiding with Him as submitted sons. Our new outlook should be to overlook ourselves so that we might see Him. Our new outlook should be to overlook ourselves so that we might see Him. The new nature recognizes that without Him we can do nothing and that we are helpless without Christ. Such a mind-set was impossible for the old nature, but now we are taught to recollect spiritual truths concerning ourselves, that knowing the facts about what Christ has made us is the basis for victorious living.

Brothers, something is wrong when I am not taught to run into Jesus during times of difficulty, but just to remind myself who I am. The spiritual life does not stem from learning the facts about my new self, but rather forgetting about myself when I look at Him. Looking at my identity causes me to look away from Him.

The new nature should be captivated by Him, by hearing His voice and experiencing His presence in daily life. The last thing the new nature will do is talk about itself, for even the Holy Spirit will not testify of Himself, but only of the Son. As a matter of fact, our new outlook should be to overlook ourselves so that we might see Him.

The only source of life is Jesus, and the perpetual gaze upon Him is the all-sufficient universal solution for everything in the life of a believer. Christ will not share the throne of your heart with you.

I am not saying that this wave is satanic or devilish, but I am saying that it is dangerous because it reminds me of a distraction that took place before the beginning of time. Lucifer, "perfect and beautiful," was the handiwork of God. As an anointed angel, God placed him as ruler over the earth. But when he began to exalt what God had made him, he was banned; he began perfect, and self-focus was enough to disqualify him from the glory of God.

Vance Havner said, "If Christ didn't come to save us from self-infatuation, I don't know what the Savior came to do." He didn't save us from self-infatuation to bring us into a sanctified form of the same. David Popovici, one of the greatest men of God that I know who is currently giving his life to preach the Gospel in hostile areas, once said to me, "It seems in the lives of many Christians that the self-life is still king; he just changed his outfit."

Michael Koulianos, founder of Jesus Image, taught on first love, saying, "I never come out of prayer thinking how great I am, but rather I can't believe He wants me." This is the beauty of His love, not that we were worth something, but that we were worth nothing, and He still died because He saw value in our worthlessness.

Even ministers I deeply respect are subtly shifting their focus. The other day, a minister that has greatly touched my life said, "When the I AM takes residence in you, you are able to say, "I am...," teaching that the evidence of God's presence is a revelation of self. This is askew. The evidence of the residence of the I AM is a life that proclaims, "HE IS."

Moses' encounter with the I AM produced a greater dependency on God: "If You don't go with me, I don't go"; and when his face shone with glory, "he knew not." Gideon was called "a mighty man of valor" simply because he didn't see himself as one. Paul wrote in 1 Corinthians 4:5, "We preach Christ, not ourselves...." A great man of God once told me, "Many people cannot recognize God's presence because they are too busy recognizing their own presence."

There are many examples of this mentality in the midst of the Western church that I could point out, but rather let me just state what we need to see: Jesus is all. Anything that is preached or emphasized to pump us into frenzy about what we are in God is distorted identity. Pure identity in Christ is Christ. True identity in Christ is the exaltation and proclamation of Christ's great worth and glory.

After searching the Scriptures, I see that there is very little reference to self-awareness in the new life. We are not taught in Paul's letters a recollection practice any more than a doctor would tell a woman who wants to have children to remind herself she is pregnant. The only way to conceive the things that God wants to birth into the earth is to intimately experience Jesus. It is a life of coming unto Him that causes us to produce fruit.

In an intimate experience with my wife, the last thing I would do is confess to myself who I am. Rather, I would allow myself to be captivated by her beauty and preoccupied with my desire for her. This is our identity—a people endlessly preoccupied with God Himself.

Today I remembered this statement: "Men quickly fall in love with their own legacies." This statement seems to be truer among Christians than anywhere else. We claim to be driven to "make an impact," but the closer you draw to our hearts, it seems to cover the lust for our own name and legacy. Our selfish humanity leads us to a hidden desire and a secret passion for our own personal significance. True identity in Christ is the exaltation and proclamation of Christ's great worth and glory.

We constantly announce our activities, results, and stories in our own ministries, but in reality we are just manifesting our Adamic pursuit for significance. I understand that the only way to tell people what is going on is to tell them what is going on, but it seems that under the guise of "identity in Christ" and "being fruitful," we have found a justification for exalting ourselves.

Does our faith rest upon what we think ourselves to be in God, or are we content to remain nothing before God that He may show Himself strong? If this is accurate, this just indicates our failure to be wholly satisfied with His sweet presence in us, with just being His, and with loving Him and receiving His love every day.

VII

ENJOYING THE GOSPEL

28

THE VISION OF THE TRENCHING SHOVEL

IF THERE IS A ROOM IN THE CORRIDORS OF GLORY, IN WHICH Christ collects things precious to His heart, I am most certain that He has not gathered sermons, testimonies or snapshots of a man's ministry highlights. If Christ were to take me by the hand into that precious room, He might take me to a trenching shovel. I might look at Him and say, "What is this?" To which He would smile and reply, "This is the shovel upon which your tears fell as you worshipped Me in the heat of the day surrounded by devils; you were without one ministry opportunity, without any personal ambition but to love Me. Do you remember? I remember."

I believe God has placed value upon things that seem insignificant to men. It seems that He will establish those who give themselves so completely over to Him that they are no longer concerned with ever being established at all. He holds precious to His heart a life of intimate communion with Him that seeks nothing but Him. He cherishes a life that isn't motivated and inspired by "service" or "results" but is completely satisfied by His whisper and nearness, even in the midst of the mundane things in life. As C.S. Lewis simply but brilliantly stated, "God doesn't want something from us, He simply wants us." Dear reader, can I submit to you that God's ultimate desire is your heart?

The church needs to have a whole new perspective of what God deems a worthy response to His indescribable sacrifice. In these days that we live in, to enjoy the gospel seems like a foreign concept. We are overcome with our desires to see results and frustrated by our attempts to accomplish giant feats for God. I am not against massive results and or grand vision at all. However, it is imperative that such endeavors have their origin in and are sustained by the secret whisper of His presence.

One of my dearest friends in the entire world, Daniel Kolenda, is one of the most successful evangelists to ever live. At the time of this writing he has not only personally witnessed over 10 million people come to the Lord by way of mass crusade evangelism, but he has watched the gospel heal thousands of irreversible sicknesses and disabilities including multiple dead people coming back to life. Even with all these successes, he showed his true heart by these words: "After the crowds have come and gone and hundreds of thousands have been won to the Lord, I sit on my bed in that hotel room and it is still only God that satisfies."

I am not trying to stop believers from accomplishment; rather I just want to emphasize that anything that has significance to God must issue from Him, His presence, His voice.

The true heart of the matter is the enjoyment of this glorious gospel: the King of Glory offers His own blissful and empowering presence to men. We must understand that such satisfaction is not merely a perk of God's presence in our lives but rather the means by which He frees and empowers us to obey Him. A Church that is not satisfied with God testifies to the world that God is not enough.

29

THE OFFERING OF GOD'S PRESENCE TO MEN

AFTER THE DEVASTATING DEATH OF THE MESSIAH, ALL THE disciples fled, just as Jesus told them they would. Three days later, Mary Magdalene went to the tomb alone and made the earth-shattering discovery that the stone had been rolled away and the tomb was left empty. In the midst of what was probably absolute emotional confusion, she saw who she thought was the gardener and asked him where he had "taken her Lord" (John 20:13). When Jesus said her name, she immediately knew that it was Him and she wanted to throw her arms around Him. But Jesus said something very interesting to her, something that has perplexed me for a long time: "do not cling to me, for I have not ascended." (verse 17)

I believe that understanding what Jesus communicated through this statement is very important to experiencing and enjoying the fullness of the gospel, for the Gospel in its completeness includes the fact that He ascended into Heaven. The reason that He tells her that He did not want her to cling to Him was because He had "not yet ascended;" this should immediately turn our attention to the reason He would ascend in the first place, which will show us the reason why He forbade her from clinging to Him.

Jesus told the disciples that "if I do not go, the Spirit will not come" (John 16:7). John 7 tells us that the Spirit had not yet been given because Jesus had not yet been glorified, which took place when He ascended. It is safe to say that the primary reason for Jesus to ascend was to be glorified and to send the Spirit. How amazing that Jesus would ascend to send!

It seems that, like Mary, much of modern Christianity has chosen to cling to the excitement of knowing the forgiveness of sins, to the joy of burying our old life and rising up in the new life we have in the death and resurrection of the Son. But Jesus would not have us embrace Him as the crucified and resurrected Son alone. He longs for something far more than just the forgiveness of our sins, the renunciation of our old life, and our walking in a new life. These are only the foundation upon which the fullness of the Salvation He purchased for us is built.

Dear reader, God's desire is to fill you with Himself. Every void in man God originally intended to fill with Himself. If Salvation is anything, it is God saving us from life and eternity apart from His presence, so He sent His very own

Spirit into our hearts. It is this Holy Spirit that is God's presence in the world today. God gives His person and presence to us in the most intimate way: He fills us on the inside and mixes with our being so that we may live in union with Him; He wants to live through us by us living by Him.

The Gospel is incomplete without the sending of the Spirit into the hearts of men. I would venture to say that this is the heart of the Gospel, because the happiness and power in our lives comes from the Spirit of God who is the presence of God. Yes, it is 100 percent true that Jesus died in our stead to take away our sins by His blood. Yes, it is 100 percent true that He was buried to lay in death our old self. Yes, it is 100 percent true that He rose from the dead so that we may rise in newness of life with Him. But it is equally true that He ascended so that we might receive His Holy Spirit into our very being. This is the complete Gospel.

Please hear my heart cry as you read these words: *the gospel is the offering of God's presence to men.* His Spirit is everything! Without Him nothing lives. If we walk with Him we will not rebel against Him. If we do not walk with Him, we can only rebel against Him. He puts right desires in us by His Spirit. He, by His Spirit, causes us to walk in His own ways.

30

EXPERIENCE

IN SPEAKING ABOUT EXPERIENCING THE GOSPEL, LET ME BE AS candid as I possibly can: *Nobody gets pregnant holding hands;* it is simply impossible. There must be an intimate encounter and physical transference in order for conception to ever transpire. Many Christians, if not most, are literally holding hands with Jesus side by side, yet there is very little to no real intimate experience of Him; true reception of His word in the sweetness of His presence is rare.

So many merely have new lifestyles and new terminology; meet with new friends and listen to different music; struggle with the things that we used to as heathen and feel bad when we sin, this is due to a lack of a deeper sense of God in our everyday lives. I am afraid that too many are content to experience Him only in the public place, but conception only happens in the private place. If I could speak even more candidly, there are certain things that I will only do with my wife when we are alone. So it is with the heavenly bridegroom: He will only perform certain things when the door is shut and the heart of His beloved is fixated only on Him.

Many people wonder why they are not pregnant with

God's purposes, or why they cannot give birth to those dreams that come from His heart. They are perplexed as to why they cannot overcome sin or see the fruit of the Spirit consistently in their lives. The sad fact is that even in the midst of the "intimacy movement," many have merely adopted the language but will not truly live a life that is centered on His presence. But just as a pregnant woman cannot hide the fact that she has been with a man, union with God cannot be hidden. And no one can reflect a light brighter than what they have actually seen themselves. We must experience Him ourselves.

It is important to note that *no one gets pregnant reading "What To Expect When You're Expecting."* Just in case you are not familiar with this book, it is a large volume on the effects of being pregnant. A woman could memorize such an in-depth work but it will never inseminate her. There are many believers who live this way: they think that if they memorize and study the Bible, they will somehow find union with God and receive the infusion of His divine substance. It is purely impossible. Man needs to receive God's Words through the Scriptures and other means such as visions and impressions, in the sweetness of His presence alone with Him, where no eye can see.

It should go without saying that *no one gets pregnant by telling themselves that they are pregnant.* But we have whole movements based upon reminding yourself of who you are in Christ, speaking things into being, or simply "right believing." Our mental acrobatics cannot perform the miracle of sweet intimacy with Jesus. It seems that our human mind will come up with anything to substitute a genuine face-to-face love exchange with God in His presence.

No one can get pregnant by desiring a child. Desire alone will never create union or the miracle that results from that union. Let me just add here that having children is not the *purpose* of intimacy but the *result* of intimacy. In the same way, God is intimate with us because He loves us, not so that we would produce offspring. We must consider that the inevitable result of intimacy will be productivity, but it is never the purpose. Intimacy unites us with Him so that our works issue out of what *we are through union with Him*.

If fruitfulness were the purpose of intimacy and not the result of this love union, than God would not be looking for a bride; He would be searching for a surrogate. On the flip side, if man looks to God for power and results alone, then ministry has become a mistress instead of his offspring of love union with His God. Everything in God is all about the mingling brought by the sweet intimate reception of His word in the bliss of His presence.

No one will become fruitful in this life simply because he or she has a great desire to be. There are whole movements based on "crying out" and fasting1 and frustrated pleading with God for something to happen. But, dear reader, this is so important for me to pass on to you: the interactive fellowship with the Spirit is our uniting experience with God, not our desire for it.

Along the same lines, *no one gets pregnant by commitment alone;* otherwise, my wife would have become pregnant the moment we said, "I do." God has given us such great parallels in our daily living of the life He wants to share with us, and marriage is a powerful one. But commitment to someone doesn't automatically mean that you are intimate with them. Though commitment is a beginning, it is still possible to be married and not be intimate.

Let me interject here that the reason why so many people know very little about the ecstasies of God is because they have no commitment to Him. Fornication is sin because it is the expression of covenant without covenant. In essence, we are telling God that other things are more important to us than our relationship with Him. Before God will overshadow you with the blissful intimate experience of His nearness, there must first be a settling in a man's heart that *all other loves are refused*. As is stated in marriage ceremonies all over the world, "...forsaking all others, keeping only to thee." God will not pour His Spirit into a man who is not fully His.

Yes, commitment is fundamental but some people really believe that because they are willing to die for Christ and His cause they are becoming like Him. But this is not the case; a man needs the presence of God to unfold the living voice of God into His soul. And those whose lives are truly His will give themselves to experiencing Him every day.

Lastly, *no one can become pregnant by knowing the "methods"* by which to do so. Without getting too explicit, one can know every way to be intimate and yet not experience intimacy with another person. Just because we can teach about prayer and have learned everything concerning the intimate life, it doesn't mean that we are living by that ecstatic experience ourselves. Experiential union comes from experiential fellowship alone.

This is the desire that burns in my heart: for the church to come into a deeper awareness, consciousness and experience of God's presence in their daily lives. There is simply no substitute for it. So let me say that quote from Mike Bickel one more time, "experiencing God is not an option." This issue is life and death. A life of experiencing God is authentic salvation. This is the abundant life.

31

LIFE

Jesus said, "Man will not live by bread alone, but by every word that proceeds out of the mouth of God." (Matthew 4:4)

IN OTHER WORDS: BREAD = WORD = LIFE. HE, AS THE BREAD of life, is that Speaking from God that must be received as our life source. John the revelator calls Jesus the "Word of Life" (1 John 1). Our life source is His speaking/voice. He is the living Speaking of God and our nourishment for a godly home, relationship, mouth, heart, employment, ministry and life. Without His voice, we are empty and lifeless. David said, "If you are silent to me, I will become like those who go down to the pit" (Psalm 28:1). The digression of every Christian life starts at this point, with the loss of His voice.

Ask yourself, "Do I hear Him in my life?" Let me illustrate the major difference between learning and hearing with this example: I used to prepare crab legs in the kitchen when I worked at the Pelican's Perch in Pensacola, Florida, but I couldn't tell you what one tastes like because I have never eaten one. You see, all the facts in the world about cooking crabs and all my outward contact with them in preparing them for others to eat never acquainted me with their taste. So it is with experiencing God; theologians across the globe have defined Him but they have never eaten Him. Because of this, their heads are heavier than their hearts; while their brains are full their souls are hollow.

"Religion," in the negative sense of the word, is lifeless devotion to God. It is seeking to live in a way that pleases God by our own efforts. Dietrich Bonheoffer once wrote, "Adam's curse was having to live life before God without life from God." Men cannot live for God without life from God. Religion is the slavery of efforts and striving; it is and will always be focused on "might and power." But true Christianity is a Spiritual thing and cannot be lived through the energy of men. We must eat Spiritual food if we are to ever live a Spiritual life. Religion is cold, dry, dead and empty; men suffocate under its power, for it presses upon men a Spiritual standard without any Spiritual power. I will say this phrase until I pass into the next life: religion demands for men to live according to a nature that they do not posses.

32

PRESENCE

The phrase "Come to Me" in its most basic understanding means entering into His presence. Jesus calls to everyone suffering under the weariness and heaviness of this life so He can offer us relief and rest. It is clear to me that our weariness in this life has its roots in the lack of His presence, and our heaviness is rooted in self-reliance. A life of rest from fear, worry, pain, striving, sin, and oppression is a life of continually coming unto Jesus. Note that all of our weariness will melt away when we come to Him.

The presence of Jesus frees us from the constant stress that the tick of time puts upon the soul; this is called rest. The presence of Jesus frees us from the constant frustration of desire that brews in the soul; this is called rest. Our senses are constantly bombarded by our surroundings but the presence of Jesus frees us from their influence; this is called rest. It is in the presence of Jesus that we are free from striving and we realize that God will perform all things through us. This is called rest. Rest is the ceasing of natural activity for the ignition of divine activity. The life of rest is the life that waits to be empowered by God's living Word. Obedience is when a man's life is yielded to the extent that God can perform through that man the things He has spoken to that man.

This heavenly bliss and freedom in His presence is not a lottery; it is rather a promise. Jesus died for our sins and was beaten for our sickness, but He came and died to close the distance between ourselves and God. It is the work of the cross that makes this wonderful and cognizant presence available to us.

33

COMMUNION

The single most common question that I am asked, both in my travels and through social media, is, "How do I experience God?" Many times I will give the inquirer a short answer like, "The experience of God is so rare because scattered minds are so common. Get still." Or I'll respond with: "Just adore Him." The reason I can address the question with blanket statements like these is because our problem is a common one: We are a self-conscious people; everything in each of our individual little worlds revolves around us.

To give God all of our attention and affection will rip the soul away from the rule of self-consciousness and set it free to fly. Most people never soar in the heights because they are weighed down by the heaviness of self-rule. The soul's rebellion must be suffocated daily by wholehearted adoration through stillness. Oh mark these words in your soul; *stillness is the antithesis of rebellion.*

So many of us go into prayer and never actually touch God because we did everything but adore Him. Many people's spiritual senses are numbed in the closet by all the pressure they put on themselves to be there and accomplish something. Our itch to accomplish something stems from our desire for something other than just Him. I would read that last statement again.

Many have also asked, "How long should I pray?" Such a question is so difficult to answer because I know that man thinks clock while God thinks connection. We all have different lives and different schedules that God has entrusted to us in this life; some have more free time than others. Nevertheless, sitting with God is the most important thing in our lives.

VIII

CONVERSATIONS ON DIVINE LIFE

34

THE PRESENCE OF GOD IS IN THE PRESENT

ATTENTIVENESS IS SO HUGE IN SCRIPTURE. PROVERBS 5:1 SAYS, "My son, do not forget." One day I had an experience when I couldn't see these words in my Bible because they were covered with gold dust. I had to push the gold dust out of the way to read them. This is so important to God. He was drawing my attention to their importance. "My son, do not forget..."Proverbs 4:40 says, "My son, give me your attention..." I remember Bill Johnson once said, "Whatever you give your attention to grows." So the lust of the flesh and the spiritual life are both increased by the same means: attentiveness.

The presence of God is in the present. It's in no other place. You cannot access the presence in the past or the future; you can only get it right here in this present moment. So the presence being in the present is how we walk in the Spirit, the consciousness that is right now in this very moment.

[We are] talking about exaltation and attentiveness connected with what God wants from us and what the devil is trying to take from us. It says in Psalm 46:10, "Cease striving and know that I am God; I will be exalted." The exaltation that He speaks to is only found in the stillness. When a man stills himself and exalts the Lord, this is where the knowledge is, where the quickening comes from. It even says in verse 11, "the Lord of hosts is with us." It's the presence all day long.

I love even the words "I AM", which are in the present tense.

35

ANOINTED ONE

Christ is the Greek word for the Hebrew word "Messiah", which means the "Anointed One". Anointing means, "smearing" and represents the presence of the Holy Spirit, symbolic in the oil, smeared on the head. Significant is the fact that in the Old Testament, only three types of specific individuals were anointed: prophets, priests, and kings; so when Peter says, "You are the Christ," he is declaring that Jesus is the prophet, priest, and king. The prophet becomes the message of God to men; the priest represents men before God; the king rules over the land and his subjects. This is what we need a revelation of: that Jesus is the Anointed One, smeared by the Spirit in these three aspects: He represents God to me as Prophet, He represents me to God as Priest; and He reigns over my heart as King.

So a man who says that He has a revelation of Jesus but doesn't accept the rule of Jesus does not have a true revelation of Jesus Christ. Doesn't Paul say (2 Corinthians 11:4) that another Jesus can be preached? We could accept a Jesus other than the Christ, but only Jesus Christ is the King who rules over everything; only Jesus Christ represents me to God as

Priest; only Jesus Christ is the Word of Life, the Prophet Himself, embodying what God is saying. We need to make sure that both of His names stay together.

I think that's the issue with other people groups, like the Mormons you already mentioned, who claim to carry the revelation of Jesus. The Scripture explicitly tells us that anyone who would deny Him to be the Son of God would be an anti-Christ (1 John 2:22). So to suppose that we carry a revelation of Jesus (even to include it in the movement's name: The Church of Jesus Christ of Latter-day Saints) but to deny Him as the Son of God, to deny the divine life of the Son, is to operate under antichrist according to Scripture. This is no small statement, so defining Him correctly, having the right revelation of Him, is essential. Jesus entrusting Himself to us and our truly living in the place of His divine life is everything.

There are growing movements, even among our own friends and influences, that won't receive Jesus' words. I think their code of belief goes something like this: "Don't get stuck in the red letters." In other words, don't focus so much on Jesus' gospel but concentrate on Paul's gospel; Jesus preaches the law on steroids (i.e. looking at a woman with lust is already committing adultery in your heart) while Paul preaches the gospel of grace. The tenet of this movement implies that Jesus' words are not meant to be obeyed but are only there to frustrate you into leaning on Paul's gospel.

36

DELIGHT WILL SWALLOW DISCIPLINE

WE PRACTICE DISCIPLINE IN SO MANY DIFFERENT TYPES OF WAYS, so generally I define it as doing the thing specifically required in the moment that you don't want to do in order to get something that you want. For example, you exercise because you want a healthy, fit body; you discipline yourself by initially putting your body through possibly unpleasant things in order to eventually get the desired result. Paul said in 1 Corinthians 9:27, " I discipline my body and bring it under strict control, so that after preaching to others, I myself will not be disqualified."

He is looking for the approval that is specifically connected with standing before the King and receiving a crown. It's interesting to note that a crown isn't valuable for what it actually is as much as for what it implies, like success or authority. In Paul's case, it stands for, "...well done, good and faithful servant" (Matthew 25:21).

I believe there is a place for discipline, and to a degree it should be practiced in every Christian life. When you study the Christian mystics, you see that they practiced deep spiritual disciplines such as meditation and constant prayer. But when we truly experience Jesus, then delight of being in His presence takes over and causes us to forget the cost of the discipline. For instance, I don't have to discipline myself to be intimate with my wife because I desire to be with her; in any situation, my heart is willing to lay itself down for her. The only case in which I would have to discipline myself to be with her is if I happened to be satisfying myself somewhere else away from her.

As beautiful as my wife is, Jesus is the most attractive being inside and outside of the universe, and as I find my delight in Him, that delight will eclipse my discipline. The difference between discipline and delight is that discipline is a tool needed to bring us to that place of delight but delight will swallow discipline if we let it.

37

OUR FATHER

My dad asked me one time, "What do you do in that room all day long?" I told him, "I drink wine." That's literally the essence of prayer; prayer is the experience of the person. Without the Presence, it's not communion.

So many think prayer is only words. But it isn't words, it's "a state of the heart", according to Henry Scougal. Prayer is so much richer and deeper than speaking Madame Guyon wrote that, "Prayer is the application of the heart unto God." Jesus said, "When you pray, [then] say..." The speaking comes out of prayer, but prayer is not only words; it is literally our internal intercourse with God, "...intercourse of our spirit with God," as Evagrios Ponticus said.

The beautiful flawless teaching on prayer by God Himself continues, He states, "When you pray, say, Our Father..." It is crucial to remember that if you have surrendered your life to Jesus, you are a child of God, always accepted no matter what your state of heart is. You are always wanted and always accepted by God no matter where you are in life. This is a major barrier—people stay away from God because they think of all the things they've done wrong, remembering the issues in their heart, and they ask, "How can I come to God when I've got all this filth and dirt on me?" No friend, that is why you need to come to God. We don't come to God because we are holy, we come to God so that He will makes us holy. We must recognize that Jesus specifically pointed out this phrase, "Our Father." You must remember that you are wanted like a son is wanted by his father.

After you recognize that you are desired by the King of kings and the Lord of lords, then we must enter into worship. "Hallowed be Thy name." It is so easy to enter into worship when we know that we are in a place where we are wanted. And it is so difficult to enter into worship when we are wondering if He is shunning us. These are the entry points into the type of prayer Jesus spoke about. Before we can say "Thy Kingdom come, Thy will be done on earth as it is in heaven, we must say, "My Father, holy is Your name; I worship You." And I believe that here, in this adoration, is the secret to prayer.

IX
NAKED TRUST

38

PRESENTING THE LORD

I HAVE FOUND IN MY LIFE THAT IT IS MORE IMPORTANT THAT He has my *attention* than me knowing what to do. I think that this concept works its way into every area of life. There are often situations where there is a temptation to not be yourself. But I felt like the Lord said to me that if I change who I am, I cannot accomplish the purpose for which He put me here. And I think that goes for many things in life. You are right where you are because *you are who you are*.

I feel I need to *present the Lord* in the way that He has *presented Himself* to me, it's a deep conviction that I carry. So, I can only give to you what He has given of Himself to me. I feel it is very important to say this because people ask me all the time, "Why are you so mushy, why are you so lovey when you speak about God?"

It's because every time He comes to me, He rushes in like a knight in shining armor rescuing me again, and again, and again! He comes in, and He treats me as if I'm the only one in the room. He is so kind, and He is so full of love. I'm telling you, He looks at you as if there is nobody else. You are a lily among thorns to Him, and He is captivated by you. There is nothing that brings His heart more joy than when you are captivated with Him too. These truths, when realized, begin to strip away our lives of anything that keeps us from Him.

As we begin a journey of stripping away all and entering a place of *naked trust*, pray with me:

I come to You, oh precious Love of mine. Your lips drip with honey and Your kiss is like wine. Your eyes are so tender, and Your voice is always kind. Your touch is bliss to me... I leave everything else behind. I'm Yours Lord, and You are mine. Everything in You I find. You give flight to the butterflies in my soul. It's You who soothes me and You who excites me. You spread joy like rain inside me. Lord, even when I'm shattered, all of my pieces they fly to You. You are most lovely to me.

All that I'm asking is that You would open our ears to hear the sweetness of Your tender voice, because it cuts and it changes and it builds and it lifts us up to be with You. Amen.

39

AM I ENOUGH FOR YOU?

IF THERE IS *ANYTHING* THAT HAPPENS TO YOU DURING THIS BOOK, let it be a bursting love from your heart toward God. A love that, only, only, only desires Him. A love that declares He is far above even the things that surround Him. God longs to be longed for. He's seeking to be sought. And throughout all of your days He will be peering into your heart to find out if you still want *only* Him. With all the things that come to you in your life and all the things He adds to you through blessing, because He is good — He asks you again and again, in the core of your heart, "Do you still *only* want Me?" I feel as if the question that is coming out from heaven is God asking, "Am I enough for you still?

I feel as if His heart is reaching out for each one of us to answer this question with sincerity, "Is God really enough?" Just God. It's so important. It's going into the motives and the intentions of our hearts.

There is something that happens when He is enough. He kills competitions, comparisons and frustrations, disappointments and offenses, betrayals and hurts, bitterness and resentment, questions and unbelief. They are all solved with one simple, "Lord, You are enough for me; not just now but for eternity. I desire you Lord, and *only* You. There is nothing else."

I'm sure that you have found, and you will continue to find, that every single situation in your life, no matter the nature of it, brings you face to face with whether or not God is still enough for you.

You say, "Eric, what I'm going through has nothing to do with God." No, it has everything to do with God! "No you don't understand. People are betraying me, people are being harsh toward me, and there are situations of sin and dysfunction happening around me." Every single one of them will bring you back to face this question: is God still *enough*; is He *only*? This is what He is longing for.

We search high and low for answers and His answer is always Him. We search high and low for answers and the answer will always simply be *Himself*. Every revelation is just Him unfolding Himself again. So you find that you hit these road blocks in your life. And when you get there you find that you are in need of a revelation. And then He comes in and He says, "It's Me. What are you looking for? Well, it's Me. If you'll understand who I am, you'll realize that you can't find anything outside of Me, everything there is, is inside of Me." God has locked Himself up in the person of Jesus Christ so that there is *nothing* of God that is accessible *outside* of Him. And everything of God is accessible only in Him. God is saying, "Am I enough? Am I enough for you?"

40

WHEN GOD IS SILENT

In 1 Samuel 11:6, the Spirit of God came upon Saul mightily to deliver the people. Saul stood up in front of everyone seemingly as God's man. Saul is exalted by the people with an undeniable anointing and a demonstration of God's power that is on his life. The glory of God seemed to be on him. God was accomplishing His purposes through him. In 1 Samuel 13:4, news about Saul spread everywhere. God has a man, God has a man! Word is traveling fast that God's got His Spirit on a man. He's going to be king. He's God's extension in the earth. This is God's guy. And then 1 Samuel 13:5 comes. A host encamps against Saul, and this is where Saul begins to change.

A host encamps against him... *this* is called pressure. It's an army ten times the size of his own. Physical weapons are surrounding him. All the people are looking at him. There's commotion. He's surrounded. Everyone looks and asks, "Saul, what do we do?" The pressure is real. What you do when God is silent is the greatest revealer of what really has your affection and your attention. Saul is looking around. God is nowhere. The Word of the Lord has not arrived.

He knows that he is supposed to wait, but pressure has a way about it. It makes you start thinking about other things. So under pressure, Saul could only see his present situation. Under pressure, Saul could only see what was *right in front of him*.

So many people cry out to God for deliverance. In Hosea 11:7, God says that His people cry out to Him, but they will not adore Him. Many times it is the deliverance men seek and not God Himself. Saul waited for a little while until he saw deliverance was not coming. Which shows us that Saul wasn't waiting for God at any point. He wasn't attentive to God at all. He was thinking about the deliverance of his situation.

In other words, what Saul is testifying by not waiting is, "God you are not enough for me; I want something else from thee." Are you understanding? It isn't about merely giving your attention to what you can get, but giving your attention to the One who's worthy of it.

41

HOLY COMPLACENCY

I'M TRYING TO GET TO THE HEART OF THE ISSUE. YOU CAN GO lay down your life in some other country, but even if you give your body to be burned, and you don't love Jesus first, it's worthless. It has to come from a heart that is captivated with His Person and not just some fascination with our own legacy. Brother Lawrence wrote this, "I don't know what God has in store for me, but I feel so serene that it doesn't matter," (The Practice of the Presence of God).

There is a holy complacency. Complacency is generally a bad word in Christianity, but there is a holy complacency. You want to know what it looks like? It means to have Him is to have everything already. It means: place me wherever You wish, take me wherever You wish, say whatever You wish, I'll do whatever You wish, because as long as I have You, I have everything. You can take every- thing from me and give me God, I'll still have everything. You take God and give me everything and I'll have nothing.

Saul was weighed down by his own ambitions, his own determinations, his expectations, his reputation, and his need for explanations. The wonderful pressure of keeping all your attention on God is home to some and misery to others. Waiting strips you down to naked trust.

It reduces you to Him only. It is the true love that excludes everything else and leaves you with Him only. Men do not acquire faith, they are reduced to it. You can't just say, "I'm going to go get faith." No, you have to be stripped down to only Him again, and again and again. It is very important because in the midst of spirituality, we've got all these things that sneak their way in like angels of light. They present themselves on the outside as very spiritual things, but in the heart of it, Jesus is not there. It's very common. We must be reduced to Him only.

The other things that lay hidden in Saul's heart were exposed the moment that these things wanted to be lifted up above the Lord. You will come to this moment. You may have come to it already; and you will come to it again because life is one endless face to face with "Is God really enough for me?" I cannot say truthfully, "God is all I want," until He is all that I've got.

You can choose the stripping. It's called love. Have you ever seen someone get married? I remember my wife Brooke and I were at a wedding. It wasn't ours, it was someone else's. The minister said to the two getting married, "Forsaking all others, keeping only to thee." The words came out and went through me, and I felt as if God was saying, "Marry Me. Forsake all others, everything else and keep only to Me."

God is looking for a man that He can take near to Himself. How blessed is the man that God draws near to Himself. Oh to want Him, to desire Him, to be satisfied with Him above all things. This is life itself. You don't live until He has all of your life. And it starts with the heart. We were not created for our spouses. We were not created for children or jobs or achievements or spiritual blessings. We were created for Him and Him alone. For Him to have all of the heart is what He's been after from the very beginning.

42

BETTER THAN SAUL

God raises up those who are bowed down because when you are bowed down, you lose all desire to be raised up at all. This is the kind of thing that God loves. He's attracted to humility like this. God had found for Himself a man after His own heart in this way; one to whom God was enough. One who loved God enough to look at Him.

One who loved God enough to wait for Him. One who loved God enough to be stripped down to naked trust. Such nakedness is an invitation for which God unendingly waits. To be stripped down to nothing invites God to be all. The nakedness of only wanting Him.

The Scripture would suggest to us that David was plucking the strings of God's heart when no man could see. Saul had the people's attention, but David had God's attention.

"If you have the smile of God what does it matter if you have the frown of men?" (Leonard Ravenhill)

WHEN WE ARE SURROUNDED

God's heart was drawn to the melodies of love rising from the heart of a young shepherd boy beside still waters laying in green pastures. 1 Samuel 15:28 God says He has found someone "better" than Saul. Do you hear this language? David is better than Saul because Saul denied the Lord when a host encamped against him. But do you want to know what David did when a host encamped against him?

He's in the very same situation that Saul was in. David says, "Though a host encamp against me, my heart will not fear; Though war arise against me, in spite of this I shall be confident. One thing I have asked from the Lord, that I shall seek: That I may dwell in the house of the Lord all the days of my life, to behold the beauty of the Lord..." (Psalm 27:3-4). He's so mesmerized that his logic seems to be suspended.

War is around him and you look at David and say: "What are we going to do? We're outnumbered, we're going to die!"

David says, "I'm confident."

"What are you confident in? Do you have another army?"

David says, "No there is only one thing I want, and it's His presence. There is only one thing that I desire, and it is to behold Him."

43

SIMEON: A LISTENING LIFE

In Luke 2:25, we're told about a man named Simeon. Simeon means "listening" or "to listen." If you think about what listening actually is, in its most basic understanding, it is literally just attentiveness. And if you think about what attentiveness is, it is the exclusion of all other things but the thing that you are focusing on.

So Simeon means, giving God all of your attention at the exclusion of all other things. It's living a life of listening. Simeon lived his entire life waiting for the coming of the Lord. It is this waiting, listening, and the exclusion of all other things that is the heart of what I want to continue to express in this appendix.

The Scriptures say specifically that Simeon was waiting. But it says firstly that the Holy Spirit was upon him. Secondly, it was revealed to him by the Holy Spirit that he would not see death before he had seen the Lord's Christ, and thirdly that he came in the Spirit to the temple.

There are three things that will accompany a life that listens to the Lord and is literally attentive to Him at the exclusion of all other things:

1. The Holy Spirit will rest upon your life.
2. The Holy Spirit will reveal. You'll have revelation from the Spirit, spiritual thoughts, spiritual words, spiritual unveilings that lead to the revelation or are the revelation of Jesus.
3. Your life will be quickened and moved by the Spirit

The Holy Spirit resting on your life; the revelation that comes from the Holy Spirit, and the Holy Spirit's movement or empowerment, all come from listening. When living a life that gives God all of your attention, the Holy Spirit can rest upon you, move you, and reveal Jesus to you.

I believe Simeon is what God wants to say to you right now. And I pray that God would grant you grace to listen, to live listening, attentive to His sweet presence. And as you're attentive to His presence, in the midst of even the mundane and all the busyness of life, living listening is living in attentiveness to God.

X
———

LOVESICK

44

OPEN TO ME

"Open to me... My Darling."
(Beloved to the Love, Song of Songs 5:2)

I DON'T THINK THERE IS A CLEARER PHRASE THAT CONVEYS God's desire for His people to yield to Him than these three words, "Open to Me..." This may seem elementary, but, for Him to say such a thing to us indicates that we are responsible for His entrance. The sad fact is that in one way or another we are always finding ways, directly or indirectly, to shut Him out. What do I mean? I mean that we choose to go on in His things, His language, His power, His purpose, His gifts, His family, His realm, while no longer looking to Him as our source and center. In order for our Christianity to be "in Christ", everything must emerge from and through the presence of Christ. Whether intentional or not, many of us live totally unaware of His presence. It never dawns on us that He mourns over our lack of awareness of His presence.

It never even crosses our minds that He is waiting for us, always ready, willing and longing to be all to us. Maybe it is because we think that this figurative "door that needs to open" that "separates us" is on loose hinges and seems to close the moment you take your foot out from under it. We all tend to be easily distracted from Him. I know this about myself; I am forgetful. I am consistently confronted with many issues that stir my self-consciousness so I get sidetracked and, consequently, my heart becomes hardened from the ease and simplicity of giving Him my attention. I know that if I am to receive Him through communing with Him I must first be open to Him. And if I am ever to open to Him, it follows from turning my attention to Him.

In Revelation, Chapter 3, we see the same picture of "Open to Me." Here lives the same cry of the Bridegroom. "Behold, I stand at the door and knock, if any man hears my voice and opens the door, I will come in to him and will dine with him and he with Me."

Why do you knock on someone's door? You may answer, "so that they will let you in." True, but that follows something easily overlooked but extremely important.

The first reason you knock is to get the ATTENTION of the one inside.

Why does God knock? It is to let us know that He is here. All He wants is our attention to be pulled from everything else and given to Him. The issue with our souls is that there are so many things that try to compete with Him; our needs, wants, frustrations, hurts, decisions that need to be made and so on. But each of these must be abandoned if we are going to set our hearts to adoring Him. Oh dear reader, you who have struggled to find the sweet abiding presence of God, if you get quiet and listen, you can hear Him, even now, whispering, "I am here. I am here. Open to Me, My love. Let me in." The omnipresence of the Lord (the fact that He is always with you) shows us that the ultimate sin, self-consciousness, is living moment-to-moment unaware of His presence.

Jesus is looking through the door, reaching His hand

through whatever opening there may be, so that we might see Him. He loves for us to perceive Him. He hopes that if we can even slightly perceive Him as He reaches for us, He might arouse our desire to experience His love in communion with His person and presence. Jesus knocks. Jesus speaks.

Jesus reaches – "give Me your attention. Respond to My presence. Open to Me." Oh dear reader - who is not yet convinced of our dire need to perceive God - the implanted faculty of our spirit at our new birth is the very means by which He perceptibly communes with us, exchanging love with us, and setting up His rule in our hearts. Jesus is showing us that through this He can become our life-supply.

45

HE WAITS FOR US

CAN YOU HEAR HIS WHISPER, SEEKING TO LET US KNOW THAT He is here, longing for us to, "Open to Him"? Maybe you don't see the Lord in this way. But the humiliation and suffering on the cross is enough to show His tender heartedness towards you. Each drop of blood fell from that cross creating a symphony of His love for you.

As He hung there, His open arms pleaded with all to open to Him. Each day we must remember the openness of the Bridegroom calling to our hearts to open to Him. I remember I was in a store shopping with my wife and a song came on over the intercom. It was called "A Thousand Years." The lyric "I have died every day waiting for you" shot through me like a holy love arrow.

I went to the restroom shut the stall door and wept, I was touched by His Spirit showing me that the death of Christ daily speaks, "open to me, I am waiting for you." Just as He cannot take back His death, He has forever extended the desire of His heart for our hearts to open to Him. The communion elements are a reminder of His waiting and invitation for us to come to Him in the midst of all of our filthiness. He knows that we are wicked and that we have great difficulty in taking our eyes off of ourselves. It is this very weakness that attracts Him to us. We simply need to recognize our deep-seated depravity and cast ourselves upon Him. Even now as you read this book, see Him; hear Him. The Bridegroom's cross is the certainty of His daily waiting for you.

You may think that you have shut Him out too many times. You may think that He couldn't possibly still want you in the same way He did the first time He knocked. Oh dear reader, you misunderstand the way He is. You fail to realize the Bridegroom's tender heartedness towards His Bride. He longs for you. He looks at you. He waits for you. His knock is not restricted, for Jesus says, "if any man..."

The invitation goes out to all. The invitation goes out to you. Right now, in the midst of your issues, in the midst of your stress, in the midst of your brokenness there is a divine table that descends from heaven spread for you, for any, for whoever will yield and let Him in. "Come, ye poor afflicted ones, who groan beneath your load of wretchedness and pain, and you shall find ease and comfort! Come, you sick, to your Physician, and be not fearful of approaching Him because you are filled with diseases; expose them to His view and they shall be healed. Children, draw near to your Father, and He will embrace you in the arms of love! Come, you poor, stray, wandering sheep, return to your Shepherd! Come sinners, to your Savior! (Madame Guyon)."

46

YIELDING TO HIS INVITATION

Even as you read this now, I beg you on behalf of the Lord; do not be content just to sense the invitation. Don't be content to merely hear the knocking of His holy hand upon the door of your heart. Yield; open to Him.

He is your loving Bridegroom. Yes, just put the book down and with all sincerity and vulnerability of heart say, "Please, come in my Precious Lover. Precious Jesus, don't wait outside, come live in me. Make me Your home today and always." If you will daily give Him time to come in, I promise, He will daily sweep you off your feet and hold you in a way that will heal and fill your soul in areas you didn't even know needed healing and filling. His touch will forever damage you beyond repair. He will unite Himself with your soul in a highly experiential way. I am learning over and over that in yielding we may look like fools, but that is the life of the lovesick. A holy Bride is wholly His.

For those of you who are unfamiliar with what I am saying, let me practically talk you through this.

Abandon all other things and turn the gaze of your soul upon Him. Once you sense the slightest impression from His

Spirit, cast off all restraint and cast yourself upon Him in absolute trust. Let Him take you; whether you are in a service, a meeting, the kitchen, or in your closet. These impressions are a heightened sense of awareness of His person through which you may pass into Him and Him into you. It is a union, an entrance into one another, a moment that carries your heart into fresh perceptions of Him. Most often, these precious sweet impressions will happen to you in times of waiting in His presence. But if they take place anywhere else, or at any other time, there is a reason. Let me encourage you, above all, do not resist Him. For stubbornness deteriorates our hearts. The definition of stubbornness is, "A resolute adherence to one's one will."

Yielding is laying your will at His feet; the resolute adherence to His will. As Madame Guyon wrote, "we cannot arrive at divine union without the repose of the will." While stubbornness says to the Lord, "I do sense You, but I am not going to let You carry me out of myself, nor out of my own controlled presentation of myself." This is why Jesus, as well as Stephen, rebuked the Pharisees. A "stiff-necked people" are a people who will not yield. The

slightest yielding to the Spirit will bring about more experiential knowledge of God's person than a lifetime of theological study or ascetic discipline. For the issue is, and has always been, the heart, "Do not harden your heart" but rather open your heart to Him in whatever way He chooses to come, just receive Him.

I once read advice from an old Christian saint of God who shook America with the power of God, "Cherish the slightest impressions of the Spirit." This is the secret of increase. Dear reader, yielding to the sweet impressions of the Spirit is the best way to cherish God Himself. Cherishing Him is the greatest stewardship of Him. This is what separates the men from the boys. The greatest saints are not those who have fasted the most, or those who know the most, or those who are loudest or most entertaining but, rather, those who have learned the beautiful death of attentiveness and surrender to God. Those who can sing back to the Lord, "I have died everyday waiting for you."

47

MY FIRST VISION OF THE LORD

The undeniable characteristic of the Bride is an ineffable enjoyment in the Bridegroom. His presence, His voice, His realm, His person - yes, the heaven of heaven is truly, the Bridegroom Himself. To bring this all together; her experience of Him has proven His powerfully attractive beauty. She exclaims, "Your whole being is breathtaking!"

If you are having a hard time understanding how this translates to Spiritual relationship with God, let me illustrate. The first time that I ever saw the Lord I tried my best to write in my journal a description of what I saw, heard and felt. I combine all three because I am not sure which one it actually was. He was unadulterated sensory overload.

My words, pen and paper are merely a feeble attempt to explain our soul's magnetic attraction to God. I wrote, "...upon what seemed like seeing Him, in that very instant every one of my desires were pulled toward Him. I was stricken breathless by the overwhelming conviction that He was unlike anything that I have ever seen before. The only thing that I could say through my tears and groaning was, "I do not want to live (here) anymore. Take me with You." For me it was the ultimate Maranatha experience. The Spirit in the Bride truly aches for His return (Rev. 22.17). Let me put this in perspective; I have a beautiful wife and two lovely daughters. My family and life are blessed and I am deeply thankful for these naturally unparalleled joys in this life. But I want to explain that the vision of Him was so magnetic that I wanted to forfeit all of it and everything in this life, forever, to simply always have Him in this capacity. Now, I know that is not at all what He wants from us and I apologize for the weakness of words, but I must at least attempt to convey the meaning of the phrase, "How attractive and enjoyable You are." He is the gravitational pull to our being.

If you pick up a rock and drop it, it is pulled toward the ground. So it is with the soul and the magnetic force towards God. He will pull it to Himself entirely. The only reason our soul will not come to Him is tolerated obstructions. If you pick up the same rock and drop it to the ground with a table under it, it will not hit the ground but stop at the tolerate obstruction. Idols and inordinate affections act as that tolerated obstruction to our vision of God and our pull toward Him. This is why John, who describes God as light and fellowship with God as walking in the Light, writes, "guard yourselves from idols-anything that would take God's place in your heart."

When we see the magnetic pull of God's glorious beauty we can understand why it is written, "rightly do they love you." In other words, "I have seen You and I totally understand how You can capture someone's heart with one glimpse." He who has seen says, "all should love you. It is right to do so." When we truly see His beauty we recognize that it is wrong to not desire Him. It is the ultimate sin for He is the ultimate beauty. In fact, all sin is a gaze away from Him. Idolatry is placing something in front of your gaze upon Him. It is a fixation upon a beauty that is far inferior to Him.

Oh dear reader, why write such things? I write them because God wants you to know that His kisses are for you. The exhilarating love of God is yours to have, to experience and to live by. His attractiveness is the antidote to this world's glitter and our personal selfishness. To see Him and hear Him, to sense Him and be with Him is the inebriating bliss of life. The fruit of which is real life giving holiness. Holy living is the unobstructed Holy One. This is why He died, to give Himself to you.

The New Covenant is the romance of the ages. Loving Him is the root of the Covenant. It reveals to us that the lack of a love experience of Him was, and continues to be, the root of our rebellion. Hence the blood that split the veil, makes a way for us to enter a face-to-face lover's exchange with Him; a lovesick blindness. The rent veil makes way for the Holy kiss. The cross opens to us the ability to surrender our lives to the kiss, the drink, and to, once again, enjoy the touch of the Lover of our souls. What else is worth living for? The true bride wants Him for Him alone. If we come to Him merely to obtain something we are not seeking Him but using Him. But in the words of Mother Basilea Schlink, "You are here. What more could I want?"

48

GOD GRABBED MY CHIN

When God taught men how to pray, He specifically pointed out two things that are essential to our experiencing sweet fellowship with Him. It must not escape our notice that He who fashioned the soul, knowing every detail of its functionality, told us to "go into your closet" and to "shut the door." This is solitude and silence. It is separation and quietness. Hidden inside Christ's golden teaching on prayer is the Lover beckoning us to "come away." The Lover of our souls constantly seeks to pull us away from everything so He can have all of our attention, face-to-face.

Once I woke up in the middle of the night because I felt someone physically grab my chin. It freaked me out. I asked the Lord what it could be and I heard nothing. Until one day, I was watching my wife working in the kitchen and I was overcome with a romantic love for her and a desire to hold her close and be alone, that I called her to come to me. She didn't listen because she was busy.

It probably wasn't the best time but I just wanted her attention for a minute. When she didn't answer me I simply walked up to her in the midst of all that she was doing and I through my arms around her and forcefully pulled her close. As I playfully held her tightly to restrain her from pulling away from me she was looking over at all the other things she still had to do. I then reached one hand up and gently grabbed her chin and turned her face towards me.

I looked in her eyes and said, "Babe, give me your attention, just for a second." She, playing along, looked at me and said, "Yes, what can I do for you?" I then just continued to look at her without saying a word. I didn't have anything to say I just wanted to receive and give the communication of attentiveness.

It wasn't until after I left the kitchen that the Lord reminded me of when He grabbed my chin in the middle of the night. Now I understood. He just wanted my full attention. He was turning my face towards Him; face-to-face, eye-to-eye, heart-to-heart. He was saying, "Come away with me before the sun rises." I also believe He was telling me that He wants to freshly captivate the hearts of His people with lovesickness again.

If you receive anything from this chapter, let it be that, no matter where you are, He wants you. No matter what has happened or how incredible your pursuit has been, He desires you beyond description. He wants your eyes on Him. He wants your ear on Him. He wants your love on Him. He wants your voice and nearness. "To Him" is always superior to "about Him" and "for Him."

49

MARRY ME

IF THERE IS ONE THING THAT I GET HIT WITH IN E-MAILS AND BY internet trolls more than anything, it's that I preach and emphasize experience far too much. Yet Song of Solomon destroys all of the arguments! This book continually pours out word-pictures blasting a loud and clear message that God is experiential. It describes God as having honey dripping from His lips! It doesn't say, "He has calloused data flowing from His mouth." He isn't a boring lover! Fire, water, light, honey, wine... all descriptions of the person of God throughout the thread of scripture, yet somehow we say He can't be felt. He is trying to tell us something. What is that something? "Taste Me! Touch Me! Experience Me! Know Me!"

The Shulamite Bride said, "Your love is better than wine." Wine is tasted, then it's received, and then it causes influence. She was inebriated with his very person. I once met a woman in Arizona who had been battered by past relationships. So much abuse and heartache had wreaked havoc on her connections with men. She came to Christ and wanted to remarry, and one day looked up to the Lord uncertainly, and asked, "Lord, who will want me?" She heard the voice of the Lord say, "Marry me!"

That is the root of what God is wanting! A people who will leap at the opportunity to experience His romantic love.

If you know anything about Jesus and walk with Him for any period of time, you know that He is distinctly romantic. God has a way of sweeping us away to experience sights, sounds, and smells of His presence and character. Suddenly, we find ourselves reminded of His sweetness and longing for more of Him.

When I was in the Brownsville revival, they used a very distinct air freshener in the church. Up until that point, I had never experienced that smell before, and for years and years after, I never experienced it again, until recently.

We went into an Italian restaurant and as soon as I walked into the restroom, I smelled the same exact air freshener from years ago at Brownsville! I immediately fell to my knees and said, "I remember, Lord! I will not forget what You did for me. I won't forget how You kissed me.

I'll live for you all of my days wholeheartedly." It's as if the Lord brings these things back up just to remind us of our affection for Him and His affection for us.

50

AN INFECTION OF AFFECTION

THE BIBLE SAYS THAT THE LOVE OF GOD IS SHED ABROAD IN OUR hearts by the Holy Ghost (see Romans 5:5). It's a literal eruption. I remember when I first began experiencing this. Something caught my eye in the first chapter of Song of Songs. She said, "Kiss me with the kisses of your mouth" (Song of Solomon 1:2). Then in chapter two, she says, "I am lovesick" (Song of Solomon 2:5).

I figure, if she is kissed in chapter one and lovesick by chapter two, then this must be a sickness caught by kisses! He spreads the sickness of love throughout the world by kissing people. Once you've been kissed by God, you cannot live unless you're kissed again! May His kiss be continually upon our lives! I often wake up in my room and rest my head against the headboard and say, "Oh Lord, even as yesterday, kiss me again that I may go on living." It's the kiss that kills the old man. It's an infection of affection!

Gordon Fee once wrote, "When a man receives the Holy Spirit, divine perfection does not set in but divine infection does."

There is no softer heart than one that lives in the kisses of

God. See, this sort of language bothers some people. I would say that you misunderstand His nature. You cannot read the book of Song of Solomon with a pure heart without coming to the conclusion that these descriptors are so very accurate in detailing our King.

When the infection of lovesickness entered my being, I didn't know exactly what was happening to me; however, I longed for more. In fact, I had such a deep desire for solitude. As did the Shulamite Bride. She said, "Meet me in the clefs of the rock in the steep pathway, all alone" (Song of Solomon 2:14).

Lovers love to be alone. They instinctively seek retreat. A retreat in which no other voice is heard and no other face is seen. A retreat in which the sights and sounds thrill the soul like nothing else. This is what He wants with you. You have to receive the love of God continually so that you can love God back continually.

It's the kiss of God that creates the bride. It's only the kiss that can make a singled eye. See, the kiss is your cure! The kiss is your call! His kiss can cure your evil and bring you into bliss! His kiss connects you back to the one for whom you sigh. There is an infection of affection for you!

The kiss kills so much darkness in the heart of men. You become His lips for mankind by being kissed by them. In Song of Solomon 2:5, we see that she says, "refresh me, for I am lovesick!" This displays that she was continually going to him for refreshment! In other words, "Without you I quickly grow stale!"

If you know anything about spirituality, you know that so quickly staleness can set into the heart! Everything might look the same on the outside. You might have the same look, the same talk, and the same exterior, yet you know that a staleness has developed in your spirit. Your call is to turn back to the reviver! Turn back to the refresher! Many people are crying out for revival, yet He is the revival!

The bride is showing us that the kiss will infect you with a lovesickness that causes you to call out for continual refreshment. People around you, in time, will begin to see that staleness will lead you into death.

Those who walked away from God did so because they first became stale. They first became stale because they stopped receiving the kisses of God. Staleness causes us to lose touch with the reality that His lips drip with honey.

The bride goes on to say, "Sustain me for I am lovesick" (Song of Solomon 2:5). She is looking to be upheld by the groom. She is looking to him for continual keeping. She essentially says, "You've got to keep me for I cannot keep myself!"

These are the symptoms of lovesickness. Lord, keep us for we cannot keep ourselves! Sustain us, God, for we cannot sustain ourselves! May an addiction to the kisses of God be birthed within us. May we be chained to the person of Jesus by our desire-filled clinging.

The bride's dependency is built on lovesickness. She is so taken with him that she is no longer the same person. We were lost before His kiss... and now we are lost without His kisses. Before He kissed us, we were completely lost. We have grown into a helpless addiction to God... and this helplessness is our safety.

XI

BURN

51

WILL YOU BE DOMINATED?

HERE I AM, AND YOU AS WELL, WITH THE OPPORTUNITY BEFORE us to choose to continue to be haunted by the lives of those who gave themselves wholly unto Jesus, or to choose as they have, to give both our life and time to the only One worth the liquid soul in our veins. Every man will one day have his final thoughts; he will turn around on life's path and see where his blood has been spent. There, in that moment, will undoubtedly be the true test of a man's love. For our lives are one long love letter to God, written today and presented to Him and read aloud before all saints of the ages and angels in glory, tomorrow.

God's desire for us is to have an unquenchable love for Jesus that results in a transformation into His likeness. As He flows into us with His life and light, our life is poured out for the world. Christianity is not about living our lives, but giving our lives. The love, with which God loved us, is the same love with which we love Him and others.

We all only have one earthly life. One fragile life made up of time, consisting of moments, and even as you read this now, your life heads toward its end.

So, as the martyr smiles at the ax, for in its shine he sees Christ's costly legacy, the coward weeps at his past, for in his tears he sees his own lethargy. He remembers his complacency, his decadency, and sees his weak, lost life, blown away in the wind, eternally worthless and insignificant. Though many people don't like to talk about this anymore, compromised Christians get nothing (Jeremiah 29:13). God wants all of your heart, because He deserves all your heart. And, He has the right to demand it, simply because He knows that no one else loves you like He does, nor can any fulfill your soul like He can.

52

SONSHIP

IF A MAN CAME TO AN ANGEL AND TRIED TO BRIBE HIM WITH money, the angel might look at him and say, "What am I going to do with that? I am from a completely other system of existence. Your money means nothing to me."

In the same way, we have entered a higher system of existence, so as to render the seductions of this worthless and therefore powerless. We don't live for our own independent lives, but by and through divine life. In fact, the two can never join together. If a man lives for his own life, he cannot partake of divine life. When a man receives divine life, he has renounced his own life.

"Man's actions should not be governed by a sense of right or wrong, but by obedience." What kind of obedience? It is obedience to the leading of the Spirit of God. "Those that are led by the Spirit are the sons of God (Romans 8). Jesus is the "firstborn among many brethren." God's desire is to "bring many sons to glory." Charles Finney said, "Cherish the slightest impressions from the Holy Ghost." Sonship is the call; "God has sown the cross into the earth to reap sons."

From the beginning, God's heart for humanity has been the same: to share with them the union that He shares with His Son. But He will form these sons by offering to them this life and giving them the opportunity to reject it. He sets before us life and death and desires for us to choose life (Joshua 24).

There are always two trees in the Garden: the tree of the knowledge of good and evil, and the tree of life. There must be two trees for the formation of character. Life is not inevitable. Oswald Chambers said, "I cannot live holy. But I can decide to let Jesus make me holy." The choice in the Christian life is to choose between being satisfied with knowing what is right and wrong and live accordingly or be quickened by a higher life and ruled by the power of the Spirit (Romans 8). Our law is the "Law of the Spirit" (Romans 8:2). This is so foreign to most believers today that it sounds like a fairy tale to tell someone that God "...will give you a new heart and a new Spirit and cause you to walk in My (His) ways" (Ezekiel 36:26).

The presence of the Spirit is a holy life. The Greek word that Jesus used to describe the Holy Spirit has many meanings. Jesus said, "The Comforter will come" (John 14). This word means: partner, teacher, leader, guide, advocate, strengthener, standby, helper, intercessor, comforter, and counselor. He performs it. Jesus, one with the Spirit and emptied of Himself, was totally sensitive to the slightest impressions from the Holy Spirit. Jesus was completely led because He was completely given to the Spirit's leading. A partial offering will never bring a complete fire. Herein lies the reason most American Christians are cold and not consumed with God—the reason why young people prefer video games to prayer and movies to the Word of God. A partial offering is never consumed. "Our God is a consuming fire" (Hebrews 12). Meaning, He only descends upon something He can totally destroy. Partiality lacks vitality. He has not ceased to be an All-Consuming Fire. He is simply "looking at barren altars with nothing to set on fire." Sonship is a human soul wholly taken up into God.

53

INTIMACY

THERE IS INTIMACY WITH GOD: "KNOW THAT HE HAS SET APART him that is godly for Himself" (Psalm 4). "The intimacy of the Lord is for those who fear Him" (Psalm 25:14). Can our finite minds grasp such a glorious separation? Can we fathom such an attachment to God? God has chosen to set aside a man apart from the others, "For Himself"?

Proverbs 8 tells us that, "I love those who love Me." Though God loves the world (John 3:16), never doubt that there is a special place in His heart and a wonderful, intimate union for those who give themselves wholly to Him. Do you recall the specific note penned out by the writer of Hebrews, quoting the Old Testament psalm, "He has loved righteousness and hated wickedness, and there- fore I have anointed Him above His fellows"? Your heart towards God can set you apart from others. In the book of Samuel, God says that He found someone "better" than Saul (1 Samuel 15:28). There is a "better," and it is connected with an obedience that is "better" than sacrifice. Hearing God and obeying Him is more valuable to God than all the religious acts that can be done for Him combined. Abraham was called God's friend (James 2:23). Daniel was a man greatly loved. Moses was the most humble man on the earth and spoke with God as a man speaks to his friend. One of the greatest statements ever recorded in the Scriptures out of the mouth of God concerning a man is about Job, "There is none like him in all the earth" (Job 1). Read that last statement again. God said that about a human. David alone was called, "A man after God's own heart" (Acts 13:22). John the Apostle was called the one "whom Jesus loved." These things are not written so that we would know they existed, but that we might aspire to be that man also.

Leonard Ravenhill said, "No one can change God's opinion of you but you." No one can love God for you. No one can seek God for you; just as no one sets my alarm for me to wake up before the sun to stare into the face of the Son. Intimacy is choosing to refuse to look into the face of life without first having looked into the face of God: "Seek my face. Your face Lord, will I seek" (Psalm 27:8).

54

ONLY JESUS

TODAY IS A GREAT DAY TO ASK YOURSELF, "AM I REALLY HUNGRY for Jesus and only Jesus?" One of the main issues in modern Christianity is that though we "love Jesus," we don't love only Jesus. A.W. Tozer, in The Pursuit of God, said that the issue in many lives is the "AND." It is the additions to God in the Christian life that snuff Him out. We live our lives and God is allowed in as a part, instead of the source of our life. David Ravenhill said, "Nothing is more likely to lead to error or heresy than to focus on part rather than the whole." I would add that nothing is more likely to lead us away from Jesus than to offer part rather than the whole.

Is Christ our life? Even in the midst of work and family, does our heart ache for Jesus? Does the All-Consuming Fire consume us? He wants to be our thirst quencher! If we would only lead people to God as the source of satisfaction, they would be led directly into life. First Peter 3:18 says, "...the just for the unjust that He might bring us to God." For He alone can satisfy the longing of the soul (Psalm 107:9).

He seeks to truly be our supreme desire! Above all else, He wants to be all-in-all to us. Do we know what we are apart from the power of God's presence in our lives? Are we burning with thirst.

Once we experience God, other fulfillments are a joke, laughable and even ridiculous next to the power of His presence that is available to us at any time. David described his thirst as a physical craving. He craved God so much that his actual body felt his longing for God.

Oh, if I could tattoo this on your soul—this is what He wants from us above everything—He wants you to be wholly satisfied with Him. He wants to be the total object of your love. "I am married unto you" (Jeremiah 3:14). He has given you His affections and commitment. "...the love of a husband is but a faint picture of the flame which burns in the heart of Jesus. Passing all human union is the mystical cleaving to the Church, for which Christ left His Father, and became one flesh with her."

With all the tenderness I have, I tell you, anyone who spends more time in front of a TV than before the Lord knows nothing of the thirst to which David is refer- ring. Anyone who wastes his time on meaningless, selfish living, knows nothing of what is pouring out of David's heart. Today, you can turn around. As you read this chapter, you can turn your heart away from vain things of time and look to Him alone.

We can tell everyone how much we "love His presence and His voice" and they may believe us, but the truth is this...most of us only love His presence when we stumble upon Him, not enough to go after Him or sincerely, relentlessly abide in Him who burns away all other things that are not Himself. Most of us say that He is life to us, but only come away from everything to sit with Him periodically. If you continually come to Him and experience the fulfillment of God, this life and all it offers will continually dissolve into nothing- ness. He alone is fulfillment. His purpose alone is purpose. The book of Acts tells us that David "fulfilled the purpose of God in his generation." It was His longing for God alone that carried Him into such an attainment. We will fulfill our purpose to the degree we long for Him. If we do not long for Him we will short-circuit the divine system for our lives.

55

PRESENTING THE FULLNESS OF CHRIST

WE MUST UNDERSTAND THAT IF THERE WAS A WAY FOR JESUS TO be Savior and not Lord, than "salvation" would never deal with the root issues in Eden (man's rebellion). The submission to the reign of Christ in the human soul is the teeth of the Gospel; the Lordship of Jesus demands the surrender to His rule. Jesus didn't come to give men forgiveness alone. Who doesn't want forgiveness? We could "save the world" just offering forgiveness. He came to reconcile men to God. Reconciliation is only a reality in submission to His rule.

For the most part, America has preached a partial Gospel; because we are afraid to puncture people, we take the teeth out of the Gospel. We must understand that to remove the teeth of the Gospel is to remove the good news from the good news. A lady said to me the other day, "God doesn't convict people to give their lives to Him in order to save them; He shows them His goodness, then they give their lives to Him." To which I replied, "Conviction is His goodness." He is so good to convict us. He is so good to take the management of our lives away from us. The man who wants to manage his own life knowing that God desires to manage it is full of selfish ambition and pride, all of which must be laid at the feet of Christ. Because, without conviction there can be no repentance, and what is repentance if we maintain the ruling of our own lives? Our identification with Christ's cross is through surrendering our hands to be nailed with His.

Conviction is a gift straight from the good heart of God. The lack of delivering the full- ness of the Gospel brings men all the way to the door but refuses to tell them how to turn the handle. We cannot fall into the trap of preaching the power of the Kingdom of God without repentance, nor fall into the trap of preaching repentance without the power of the Kingdom. To be convicted is to be brought to the place where we can actually lay our lives down at the feet of Jesus. Without conviction man only acknowledges Jesus. But to believe in response to an internal Spirit conviction is not partial or conditional. To surrender to this Kingdom is not withholding. Faith in its very essence of meaning is contrary to partiality. Paul explains to us in Galatians that any alteration by addition to the Gospel will severe us from Christ. "A diluted Gospel is no Gospel at all" (David Wilkerson).

One of the most impacting statements on this subject is from Art Katz when he said, "The idolatrous religions are those that give men a small measure of religious satisfaction yet, they allow men to retain the lordship of their own lives."

It dawned on me one day that if the devil can seduce Christianity away from the cross, he will create the most successfully "positive"—death trap that there has ever been. Paul warned about "another Jesus" (1 Corinthians 11:4) and a Jesus that isn't King, isn't Jesus. A Jesus that doesn't remove you from being the manager of your own life is not King Jesus. The greatest news in the world is that God will take your wicked-sinful- no-good management of your life and will resurrect it, giving you divine purity, power, and life. Death for life is the main principle of the Kingdom. Everything in God is gained by death. God has no obsession with death. He loves resurrection life! He can only resurrect that which is dead. Needless to say, any "gospel" that allows you to retain the lordship of your own life is no good news at all. It is not Jesus, but a manipulation of things through a message about "Jesus." It doesn't save, because it fails to enter into the reality of what salvation is.

56

THE CHURCH

THE CHURCH, AS AN AUTHENTIC SPIRITUAL COMMUNITY, IS A people of common union, sharing spiritual communion, keeping a common unity. "The Word of God never tells us to create unity but to keep it. Christ made us one at the cross."[91] The rejection of the cross will cause a rejection of each other. The rejection of each other is a rejection of the cross. "The Church is to perfect our wisdom and knowledge on how to live with each other" (Art Katz, True Fellowship).

One minister so convincingly stated, "You don't gossip about the brothers you pray for." I desire to press such an issue further and say, when you really pray for your brothers and with your brothers, in the presence of God, you will melt into them. You will genuinely care for their purpose. The house that we, as a spiritual family, live in is none other than a house of prayer (Matthew 21:13). Having been united in prayer, we will genuinely seek each other's best interest. We will genuinely prefer each other above ourselves. We melt together in the presence of God together. "God Himself is a sweet company" (Bonhoeffer) so He reproduces the same. Jesus taught us to "love one another" (John 13:34).

It is my experience that when two individuals that are flowing with God's love come together, they automatically love one another with no strings attached, because its basis is not founded upon what each one has done or can do for each other, but because of what Jesus did for us, mystically making us one, and by the example He gave us on the cross. Jealousy is foreign to such love. Competition is dissolved, and self-promotion is exchanged for the promotion of your brother. Without this kind of united spiritual love, the devil will find a way in and insert a bomb to scatter us, wounded and injured.

MY EXPERIENCE OF SUCH SPIRIT SELFLESSNESS

Years ago I was blessed to work for a worldwide organization that is currently changing the world. I got hired on as a warehouse worker without an ounce of responsibility but to keep this warehouse clean. I heard that one of my dear brothers to whom I was melted together in the fires of the revival in Pensacola was looking for work. I instantly was filled with a desire to help him in any way that I could. I wanted to help him, not out of pity or responsibility, but because I loved him. So, I soaked the situation in prayer and brought his name and résumé before a leader in the organization. He was hired on immediately.

This brother is a gold mine of a person, and I knew that he would excel fast. It was not long after that I was moved again in my heart for him. Though he was doing well, in love for him, I was moved with a desire to see him excel further into what I knew he was called to do, and I approached the CEO of the organization with a strong swing for him. I knew no one more capable of running that whole organization and taking it further than it had yet been than my dear brother. I openly spoke for him, without him knowing. Needless to say, God ended up moving the CEO's heart to not only take him in, but eventually give him the whole company.

During this time I was let go, and went into the only field of work that I could find, which was construction. And anyone who knows anything about construction knows that it is not an ideal workplace, especially for a man who wants to live holy. A few years later, I visited my dear brother when I was driving by his office one day. I can still see the scene; he had an office looking exactly as you would imagine a CEO's office of a massive multi-country organization would look.

He had a personal assistant and the world at his fingertips. There I sat in his beautiful office, while in my own life I was in a far less ideal situation, worn out and tired from constructions ways. And, being completely honest before the Lord, everything inside of me was so happy for him and proud of him that I could have cried in front of him. But I saved my tears for the car ride home. There wasn't an ounce of jealousy or competition or desire to be recompensed in any fashion. I was honestly and completely strengthened and encouraged by seeing him and his situation flourishing and moving forward.

This story is the product of divine love, the mixture of the union of the Spirit, and the effects of the cross. I could never have mustered up enough love for someone to genuinely care for them without a touch of personal ambition. That is not natural. It is the Holy Spirit. Such a love and union by the Spirit that crushes competition, suspicion, personal ambition, doctrinal differences, and personality preferences must flow through the Church. As you see, this man is taking the organization to new heights, and that was God's plan. I am humbled to have even the smallest part in such a situation.

Do you see that this is how God works? He relies on our surrender to Him to be able to maneuver things quickly. Some things take forever to come to pass because they are stopped up with envy and strife and selfish ambition. But, such a selfless love is the product of the cross. It feels strange using myself as an example of this, but I know that it had nothing to do with me. God wanted him there and God touched my wicked heart to love my brother with Godly love. All we have to do is stay fixed upon Jesus and such will be the case between each of us, if we can see that Jesus died for such a love and allow the Holy Spirit to simply perform it, by getting out of the way and laying down ourselves. Not only will it destroy the weeds that seek to choke out divine love and its product of unity, but it will also birth a super- natural longing to be together.

57

THE PROBLEM IN COMING TOGETHER

IF WE ARE NOT PERSONALLY IMMERSED IN GOD WE WILL BE OF little value to other people. If God does not consume us, when we are alone, we will not be consumed by Him together. If our personal time is spent in wasting time and the fluff of entertainment and worthless things, we will have a hard time living together in an eternal serious mind-set. The problem that I am seeing is that the Church is playing video games together instead of praying together. The Church is playing sports or watching sports together instead of preaching the Gospel together. The Church today would much rather call a poker night than a season of extended prayer and fasting for the city. No wonder there is strife and self- ambition, competition, and dissensions. No wonder divine melting love is foreign to the modern Church system. We are living like mere men instead of the spiritual conduits that we are to each other's lives.

Without genuine spiritual vitality amongst us we are not operating as a spiritual community. Without spiritual vitality we turn into a collection of friends staying out of trouble. Or a social club membership. There will be no spiritual union or divine melting through hours of movie nights or football. Community is spiritual union as we deliver Christ to each other and to the world together. A pizza night with two movies and a prayer is the evidence of an apathetic complacency that will eventually spiral into sin, division, selfishness, and death to the unity.

We tend to gravitate only toward those who are as fleshly as we are, as spiritual as we are, or gifted in the same way. May God destroy partiality and bring in a flood of divine love for one another, connecting us as brothers who do the will of God, reaching to this world in prayer, fasting, true spiritual fellowship, and preaching the Gospel.

> *"There is no other way, for the way, to be the way, than the way, the way was, when it was the way."*

The first Church was not perfect, but they shared their lives together. We are not after perfection, because we are all flawed. The perfect bond isn't flawlessness, but the protection of love toward one another that covers a multitude of sins, rebukes each other's sins, and works through each other's sins. The first fruits of the Holy Spirit's outpouring show us the heart of God for His people. I am convinced that the Holy Spirit upon our lives will create the same today. The social club ways of many modern churches is an evidence of the need for a fresh baptism of the Holy Spirit.

We must allow the Spirit of God to move us in love for one another beyond our natural tendency. We need a closer life. Many men of God have fallen because there was no brother doing the will of God by his side and burning with enough love for him to look into his eyes on a regular basis and see if his heart was compromising.

Most church systems in America today are an environment where men can satisfy a religious itch, get an ounce of

God, and hide from any real dealing with their personal issues. Not only will this never manifest the oneness that Jesus wanted amongst His own (John 17:22), but it will also cause an inoculation toward the real desire of God for His people.

58

TAKE UP YOUR CROSS

THE END GOAL OF EVERYTHING IS FOR US TO BE JUST LIKE JESUS. He is "bringing many sons unto glory..." (Hebrews 2:10). The cross is the only instrument that He uses to fashion us into His image. Our cross is not a new one just for us, but the identification with His cross through surrender. Our cross is to identify with His cross. His cross deals with our sins; our cross is the continual identification with His cross that deals with the self-life. The self-life is that selfishness that steps in the way of the wisdom of God's selflessness being demonstrated through us. God so loved the world that He gave His only Son so that whoever places his trust in Him would possess life (John 3:16, my paraphrase). Faith is the essence of everything in God.

Faith is this: the absolute refusing to trust in yourself and the casting of yourself totally upon Him. It is the cross! Faith and the cross are inseparable. They are synonymous. Why? Because faith is the resignation of yourself and the resignation of yourself is death, and total surrender is the faith of death igniting divine life! God did not nail His own hands down, but simply surrendered them to the nails. Our cross that taps us into the power of His cross, demonstrating the demon-dethroning power of God, is selfless surrender to the nails. Beware of any movement that excludes death to self. Death to self is the key to all the doors that we will enter and exit our entire Christian lives. The daily death to self is the only way to follow (Luke 9:23; Matthew 16:24). Nothing else will bring the resurrection power of the new life existence in God, causing us to demonstrate such wisdom in the world in keeping with God's eternal desire to show it through the Church to the fallen rulers, who are, even now, losing power and are about to be changed like an old garment (Hebrews 1:12).

The sad fact is, for the most part, the Church in the West has looked to everything else but the foolishness of the cross, preached in the power of the Spirit. I was in a local church, and an amazing thing struck me as I sat back and watched the presentation of the Sunday morning service. In the midst of multicolored blinking lights, coupled with smoke, a massive flat screen flashing modern art while the "worship leader" leaped onto the front pews singing into the camera, my little daughter said something to me in her innocence that struck my heart. Though I am not against using our artistic gifts to lift up the name of Jesus, this particular situation was a prophetic picture that was etched into my heart. My four-year-old daughter was mesmerized at the fast-paced busyness of the whole presentation. In the midst of it, she tapped me on my shoulder and asked a question I will never forget: "Daddy, where is Jesus?" Then, looking intently at the whole stage setup, she said to me, "There He is."

I asked, "Where?" And she pointed my attention behind all the flash and glamour, to the dark, empty baptismal tank above which hung an old rugged cross. There were no lights shining from it. There was no smoke coming from it and it wasn't spinning. It was simply hanging there in the shadows, lost in the background of this expensive light-show concert in the name of Him who died. Behind the flash, left in the shadows, was the powerful wisdom of God, unattractive to man and overlooked by all, as the eyes of seraphs and cherubs, living creatures and archangels, flood the golden ground of heaven with confused tears, wondering why man doesn't understand how holy and sacred that old wooden cross truly is.

I am simply using this experience as a prophetic picture for the Western church. It seems we have forgotten His wisdom, where the power lies, and where the glorious revelation of God is: in Jesus crucified and slain for all to see. Let us make a resolution together, "to know nothing among men, save Jesus Christ and Him crucified" by surrendering our lives to death in response to His surrender unto death, that demonstrated His wisdom and reconciled all things to Himself by a single deathblow to darkness.

59

REPENTANCE

LAST WEEK, I WAS SITTING IN A BRIGHT YELLOW WAITING ROOM, waiting for my Ford Taurus to get an oil change. While I was there, a minister who had fallen into sin a few years ago was on television. I couldn't help but watch, interested to hear his heart.

This was the second time I had seen him on TV since his moral failure, and every time I have seen him, he states that he has gone through extensive therapy and heavy counseling, and has finished the restoration process.

He is still married to his wife and finds himself struggling with thoughts of homosexuality to this day. Concerning his failure, he states the classic line, "No one is perfect and everyone makes mistakes."

No! Homosexuality is not a mistake. A mistake is when you forget to close the refrigerator door or forget to take out the trash. This was a gradual hardening of the heart that led to such a moral decline. A heart that has no conviction for lusting for a passing stranger is in a bad state; but a heart that enters a continual affair with a man is a heart that is need of a deeper work of the Spirit, especially because he was a minIster of the Gospel (James 3:1). The red flag for me was that I never heard him mention the word repentance or the power of God in his life to overcome, or most importantly, the blood of Jesus. Nor did he mention taking every thought captive to the obedience of Christ or anything about putting off the old man and putting on the new (2 Corinthians 10:5; Romans 13:14). Is this horrible mind-set alive in other Christians living in America? Is there forgiveness *without repentance*? Read these words from William Booth's prophecy one hundred years ago:

> "The chief danger of the 20th century will be religion without the Holy Ghost, Christianity without Christ, forgiveness without repentance, 'salvation' without regeneration, politics without God, and heaven without hell."

Notice in the middle, General Booth speaks of, "forgiveness without repentance." I believe in forgiveness and reconciliation to all, no matter what social class or level of wickedness they come from. But, there is a difference between what we have seen in this pastor and the repentance seen in the parable of the prodigal son (Luke chapter 15).

For those of us who are not familiar with the parable, there are two sons. The younger of the two said to his father, "Father, give me my portion of goods; my inher- itance. I am entitled to the money that is to come to me" (paraphrased).

The Word of God states that not many days after that, the younger son gathered all his things together, took his journey into a far country, and wasted his substance with riotous living. And when he had spent all of his substance, there arose a mighty famine in the land and he began to be in want. His situation got so bad that he went and joined himself to a citizen or joined himself to a total stranger of that country; and he was sent into the citizen's fields to feed pigs.

Here is a young man who was once rich and now is in poverty. On top of that, there rose a mighty famine. Things have gotten so bad that he had to join himself to a citizen of that land. Here, the word "join" means, "to cleave to or to be glued together." It has the same meaning as when a man joins himself to a woman in marriage.

At this point the young man hits rock bottom, longing to fill his stomach with the food that the pigs were eating. In the preceding verse, it states that the young man starts to come to his senses and he begins to remember his father and his father's house. He asks himself, "Why am I here starving to death?"

I believe a lot of individuals, especially the young, are starving to death, maybe not from a physical hunger, but for the Word of the Lord. They are wondering, "Are there any absolutes in life?" There is an absolute in life. It is the Word of God.

In the book of Amos, it describes that there will come a day when there will be a famine, not of food or of thirst for water, but a famine of hearing the Word of the Lord. America is at this point. "There are too many puppets and not enough prophets in the pulpits of America" (Leonard Ravenhill).

This young man heard the words of his father and he didn't cry out, "Father, I have made a mistake," or "Nobody is perfect." He cried out, "I have sinned" and "I have sinned against God." Not the Church. Not his family. But, "I have sinned against heaven and against God." Notice the same response from David in Psalm 51, "Against You and You only have I sinned." At this very point the restoration process began and the young man was restored to his father's house, and he was clothed in his right mind.

Now, back to the anonymous preacher. Not once during the interview did this pastor state that he sinned against God or against heaven. He did not, at all, seem to be concerned about his relationship with Jesus. How do I know that? Well, he didn't mention Him once. He spoke like a man who was only sorry because he got caught. I know this because his sorrow didn't cast him upon the blood of Jesus, but on a "restoration" process. My friend, this is worldly sorrow, which leads to death.

To the individual who is reading this, ask yourself, with a sincere heart, "Have I truly repented of my sins and turned to God? Do I really know Jesus? Do I really have a relationship with Jesus, not just with a church or a religion?" Jesus states that He is the way, and the truth, and the life. No one comes to the Father except through Him (John 14:6). Jesus is the door. Now I charge you to walk through Him, but before you do, make sure you COMPLETELY close the door to your past.

"Repentance must be a change of mind that produces a change of conduct and ends in salvation. Have you forsaken your sins? Or are you still practicing them? If so, you are still a sinner. You may have changed your mind, but if you have not changed your conduct, it is not Godly repentance.... False repentance is the sorrow of the world; sorrow for sin arising from worldly considerations and motives connected with the present life" (Charles Finney, You Can Be Holy).

"Jesus doesn't save you in your sins, but from your sins" (Dr. Michael L. Brown, How Saved Are We?).

"You say, 'When so and so preached, I got saved.' Well, what are you saved from? Are you saved from lying? Are you saved from cheating? Are you saved from lust? Are you saved from rebellion against your parents? Come on! What are you saved from?" (Leonard Ravenhill, Audio Messages)

60

A MANIFESTATION OF OIL

The first time that I saw oil I was in my prayer closet, and after my wife had called my name, I opened the door and began to speak with her from the threshold of the door. When I touched the threshold with my hand, oil was oozing out of the top and sides from inside the prayer closet. I told my wife to come over and feel it. She was tripping out. She smelled it and it smelled just like frankincense oil. We were both in shock and knew beyond a doubt that it was supernatural.

As I sought out the meaning, I remembered the threshold in Exodus 12. The blood was placed on it to save the life. So I knew that the threshold represented my life. According to the common typology, the oil represented the precious Holy Spirit and the fact that it was flowing only on the inside; I was able to see His message. The anointing of the Spirit flows from inside of the secret place. He was solidifying for me again this wonderful truth: "Stay with Me in the secret place and the oil will ooze out."

Now, could it have been oil that someone anointed my doorpost with at some point when I wasn't there? Maybe, but probably not, since no one goes back there but me and my family, and my six-year-old is too short to do it; nor does she know where my oil is. Could I have anointed the door myself *and had forgotten that I did? Maybe, but I don't think my memory is that bad. So to me, it was precious and a lovely speaking of God to my heart.*

ABOUT THE AUTHOR

Eric Gilmour is the founder of Sonship International—a ministry seeking to bring the church into a deeper experience of God's presence in their daily lives. He enjoys writing on the revelation of Jesus Christ in the Scriptures and personal experience of God.

Also by Eric Gilmour:

Lovesick

How to Be Happy

Mary of Bethany

How to Prosper in Everything

The School of His Presence

Enjoying the Gospel

Into the Cloud

Nostalgia

Union

Divine Life

Burn

Naked Trust

Honey

CPSIA information can be obtained
at www.ICGtesting.com
Printed in the USA
JSHW021130231121
20700JS00001B/2